N. M Redmond

Short Sermons on the Epistles for Every Sunday in the Year

N. M Redmond

Short Sermons on the Epistles for Every Sunday in the Year

ISBN/EAN: 9783744742177

Printed in Europe, USA, Canada, Australia, Japan

Cover: Foto ©Lupo / pixelio.de

More available books at **www.hansebooks.com**

SHORT SERMONS

ON THE

EPISTLES

FOR

EVERY SUNDAY IN THE YEAR

BY THE

VERY REV. N. M. REDMOND, V.F.

SECOND EDITION, 1894.

FR. PUSTET,
Printer to the Holy See and the S. Congregation of Rites.

Fr. Pustet & Co.,
NEW YORK & CINCINNATI.

PREFACE.

The motives which prompted the writing of these short sermons on the Epistles, were precisely the same as alleged for the "Short Sermons on the Gospels," which, some time ago, appeared in a small volume. These like the others were, in part, published in the Catholic journal of Sioux Falls at the request of the Rt. Rev. Bishop Marty. The purpose was to furnish weekly instruction of a religious nature to the people of the out missions, who, owing to the large territory and the scattered Catholic population of the diocese, could not, without grave inconvenience, hear a sermon or instruction, save at monthly or even greater intervals. The "Short Sermons on the Gospels" it would seem, have been deemed useful, so to redeem a promise of long standing, caused by organizing a school, these were prepared for the publishers. Pains were not spared to render them as replete as possible with matter suggested by experience, as best adapted to the wants of the people. Should they be the occasion of raising even one soul to a more appreciable sense of her duty to God, then the labor of preparing them will have gained its reward.

THE AUTHOR.

LEAD CITY, BLACK HILLS.

CONTENTS.

		PAGE
I.	FIRST SUNDAY OF ADVENT—Delay of Repentance,	9
II.	SECOND SUNDAY OF ADVENT—Catholics more than others Debtors to God's Mercy,	14
III.	THIRD SUNDAY OF ADVENT—The Blessing of a Tender Conscience,	19
IV.	FOURTH SUNDAY OF ADVENT—The Vice of Rash Judging,	24
V.	SUNDAY WITHIN THE OCTAVE OF CHRISTMAS—Catholics should esteem Heavenly Riches rather than those of Earth,	29
VI.	FIRST SUNDAY AFTER EPIPHANY—The World to which we must not Conform,	35
VII.	SECOND SUNDAY AFTER EPIPHANY—True Fervor,	40
VIII.	THIRD SUNDAY AFTER EPIPHANY—Kindness and its Effects,	45
IX.	SEPTUAGESIMA SUNDAY—They who forego God's Eternal Prize for the World's Bribes,	50
X.	SEXAGESIMA SUNDAY—Ruinous effects of Scandal,	55

		PAGE
XI.	QUINQUAGESIMA SUNDAY—The Misery of the one who Loves not God,	60
XII.	FIRST SUNDAY OF LENT—Those who Delay the Conversion,	65
XIII.	SECOND SUNDAY OF LENT—The Christian's Duty as Expressed in the Sixth Commandment,	70
XIV.	THIRD SUNDAY OF LENT—Fly the Conversations of the Evil-disposed,	75
XV.	FOURTH SUNDAY OF LENT—Freedom and Slavery before Heaven,	80
XVI.	PASSION SUNDAY—Thoughts on Our Lord's Sufferings,	85
XVII.	PALM SUNDAY—Humility as Taught by Our Lord,	90
XVIII.	EASTER SUNDAY—A True Conversion,	95
XIX.	FIRST SUNDAY AFTER EASTER—The Holy Ghost within the Soul bears witness to Christ's Divinity,	100
XX.	SECOND SUNDAY AFTER EASTER—Patience in Trials,	105
XXI.	THIRD SUNDAY AFTER EASTER—Catholics should Honor, not Disgrace their Vocation,	111
XXII.	FOURTH SUNDAY AFTER EASTER—The Vice of Anger and its Offspring,	116
XXIII.	FIFTH SUNDAY AFTER EASTER—Those who Hear but Practice not God's Word,	121

CONTENTS.

		PAGE
XXIV.	SIXTH SUNDAY AFTER EASTER—How the Friends and Enemies of the Holy Ghost will fare on Pentecost,	126
XXV.	PENTECOST SUNDAY—The Blessings of the Holy Ghost to the Soul in whom He abides,	131
XXVI.	TRINITY SUNDAY—Motives and Means for Honoring the Most Blessed Trinity,	137
XXVII.	SECOND SUNDAY AFTER PENTECOST—Reasons why the World hates the Spirit and Maxims of Our Lord,	143
XXVIII.	THIRD SUNDAY AFTER PENTECOST—Confidence in God,	148
XXIX.	FOURTH SUNDAY AFTER PENTECOST—The Thought of the Reward makes our Suffering light,	153
XXX.	FIFTH SUNDAY AFTER PENTECOST—Christ purchased Peace—how to have It,	158
XXXI.	SIXTH SUNDAY AFTER PENTECOST—Our Baptismal Covenant,	163
XXXII.	SEVENTH SUNDAY AFTER PENTECOST—Virtue and Sin—their End contrasted,	168
XXXIII.	EIGHTH SUNDAY AFTER PENTECOST—Means which sustain the Spirit against the Flesh,	173
XXXIV.	NINTH SUNDAY AFTER PENTECOST—The Wise learn from the Mistakes of the Unwise,	178

CONTENTS.

		PAGE
XXXV.	Tenth Sunday after Pentecost—Without the Holy Ghost we are Helpless,	183
XXXVI.	Eleventh Sunday after Pentecost—Christian Humility—its Necessity,	188
XXXVII.	Twelfth Sunday after Pentecost—The Ministers of Christ.	193
XXXVIII.	Thirteenth Sunday after Pentecost—The Sacred Name of Jesus,	198
XXXIX.	Fourteenth Sunday after Pentecost—Reading—Its Good and Bad Features,	203
XL.	Fifteenth Sunday after Pentecost—Those who apply God's Word to their daily Lives,	208
XLI.	Sixteenth Sunday after Pentecost—To give Glory to God, the Mission of the Soul,	213
XLII.	Seventeenth Sunday after Pentecost—our Lives should be consistent with Our Faith,	218
XLIII.	Eighteenth Sunday after Pentecost—Envy destroys Love for God and Man,	224
XLIV.	Nineteenth Sunday after Pentecost—The Evil of Lying,	229
XLV.	Twentieth Sunday after Pentecost—Drunkenness and its Christian Remedy,	234

CONTENTS.

PAGE

XLVI. Twenty-first Sunday after Pentecost—The Word a Sword—Its Good and Bad Uses, - - 240

XLVII. Twenty-Second Sunday after Pentecost—Our Obligation towards our Neighbor in Spiritual Need, 245

XLVIII. Twenty-Third Sunday after Pentecost—Imitation of the best Christian Models found in Self-Denial, - - - - - 250

XLIX. Twenty-Fourth Sunday after Pentecost—We should be Grateful to God for the Gift of Faith, 255

I.

FIRST SUNDAY OF ADVENT.

"But put ye on the Lord Jesus Christ." Romans xiii. 14.

These words of the Apostle have the same import as if he had said "be truly converted to Our Lord Jesus Christ." Though there never has been a time in our lives in which this has not been our incumbent duty, we have to-day entered upon a season which demands its fulfilment with extraordinary emphasis. Another Advent is now upon us, and our mother, the Church, in her epistles, in her gospels, and even in the color of her vestments, reminds those who have been asleep in sin of this duty. Our parish has the misfortune of members asleep in sin. No doubt they have at times become disgusted with their manner of living, and as often resolved to turn to God. But like the good resolutions on the same matter of thousands now in hell, theirs have fallen short of execution. How long will it be thus with them? Time will stop for them, they know not how soon. Would it not seem that they should learn from the wofully sad experience of others? They are on the same road; they act in the same reckless way. What, then, can they expect but to end like those whom they so faithfully imitate? Those whose example they so faithfully follow were as free from the thought of giving their souls to hell and the devil as they now are. But all the same, God they continued to provoke, just as is being done by those who imitate them, till by a just judgment they fell impenitent. They heard but heeded not the Church in this holy season, but for them the time of mercy has passed, and God's justice in hell they must ever feel. So shall it be with those who follow their example. Great God, how blind! how utterly unreasonable men are in this all important matter, when they fail to hear and heed Your voice; when they learn not from the eternal ruin of others! God's justice in eternity towards the sinner can in a manner be preconceived from His rejected mercy towards the latter in time. Now He permits Himself to be the object of the sinner's worst insult; then He will make the impenitent wretch the feeler of His most searching justice. The insults which God in His tender mercy now bears would demand from the crowned heads of earth the utmost punishment at their command. But not, as it were, till He has exhausted His mercy in suffering the sinner's insolence, in exhorting him in the strongest terms to return, in holding out to him the graces to do so, does God allow His justice to take the place of His mercy. See then, O man of a sinful conscience, what you are to expect if you persist in your iniquity! Will you sensibly say, "now I shall break with my evil ways and return to my God. How fortunate I am to yet have it in my power to do so! Long ago I deserved to be cast headlong into hell; away with any further risk." Or will you be so reckless as to delay your repentance and continue in the evil tenor of your ways? Ah, take care; if God in His tender mercy has borne with your insults and insolence in the past, you have good reason to feel how awful will be the rigors of His justice whenever it will take the place of His mercy.

Then will He say to you in the language of the Scriptures: "Because I called and you refused, I stretched out my hand, and you regarded not; you have despised all my counsels, and have neglected my reprehensions, I will also laugh at your destruction, and will mock when that which you feared shall come upon you. Then shall you call on me and I will not hear." But if now you return, all will be well. His words to you now are: "Delay not your conversion to the Lord, and defer it not from day to day, for His wrath shall come in a sudden, and in the time of vengeance He shall destroy thee." Will you still continue an enemy to God; will you leave this church to-day without any resolution of change, and spend this Advent as you have others—tempting God to strike you? If so I pronounce you a man of the most absolute folly, who cannot in your present state have peace, and refuses to receive any. You are the abject slave of your master Satan, and in your folly refuse to return to the liberty of the children of God your Father. You groan under the lash of the tyrant, but reject the comfort of freedom; you experience in your bad conscience something of the remorse of the damned, but you refuse a foretaste of the bliss of heaven in the peace of a good one. What, O deluded mortal! are your excuses for such folly?

Perhaps you will say that you are not prepared now for the difficult task of a change from sin to grace. Will you be more so in months or years to come? Shall you be better prepared after you will have added months and perhaps years of sin to those you have now to deplore? True the enemy deters you now, but with greater force will he be able to do so in the future.

Now your sad account with God is smaller than it shall be if you defer a settlement; though sorely and frequently offended now, God will be the more provoked the longer you delay your repentance, and as a consequence the firmer will be Satan's hold on you. Hence "now is the acceptable time;" you know not that the morrow will be yours, or if it will, you know not that grace will be granted you. Over time and grace man has no control; they are the gratuitous gifts of God. How many before you have tried to defer to the morrow what they should have done in their day, and will ever bewail their mistake? Were the business of conversion not to man a matter of the greatest importance, then the folly and danger of deferring it might to an extent be palliated by pretexts. But since eternal ruin can come to the man with a conscience burdened with mortal sin, no motive whatever can justify his delay. This Our Lord very clearly expresses in these words: "What will it profit a man to gain the whole world and lose his soul." The action of men who run the risk of financial ruin, even with the view of gain, no sensible man will commend. Much more should the action of the man be condemned who would risk his all without hope of gain, and nothing could justify the action of the man who in any case was certain of a loss, but, however, would take the risk of losing all. Is this not your case, O man! who refuses to settle your accounts now, when every hour from this you are certain will be to your loss, and may possibly bring you absolute and eternal ruin? You cannot possibly gain by delay, but you are certain to lose. What, then, short of sheer madness, can prevail on you to defer your conversion? Take this warning; it may be the last which the mercy of God will allow you.

All must see that the danger which threatens the sinner who defers his conversion is not over-estimated in anything I have said. It will not be out of place to remark, then, that all the friends, all who take a Christian interest in the man who has been deferring his conversion, should exert themselves as prudence will suggest, to induce him to make his peace with God. The parent should do so in respect to children, and the latter should serve this good purpose in the case of the former. The wife, as she values the best interest of her husband, should not be remiss in this duty of charity, nor if needs be, should a husband neglect a like favor to his wife. Friend should interest himself towards friend, neighbor towards neighbor, and thus try to avert the most absolute ruin that can possibly befall a human being—the loss of heaven and commitment to the eternal pains of hell.

II.

SECOND SUNDAY OF ADVENT.

"But that the Gentiles are to glorify God for His mercy." Rom. xv. 9.

God's mercy, as one of His divine attributes, is infinite, and His expression of it to man has been from the beginning infinite. Man, like the Angels, deserved as the consequence of his disobedience to the mandate of his Creator to be cast into hell, but God made him the object of His tender mercy. He cheered the poor, depressed parents of our race who had committed themselves and us to the prince of darkness, by the promise of a Redeemer Who would conduct us back to light. This promise, for it was the promise of God, was of infinite weight, and the Redeemer co-equal to Himself. Besides, every mortal offence of which man is guilty, when measured from the infinite majesty of God against which it is directed, is infinite; hence to spare the perpretrator from the doom of the rebel Angels is a new expression of His infinite mercy. When we go back and inform our minds of the vicissitudes of the human family, and note the forbearance of God with its members, both in general and in particular; when we read of the numerous and signal favors which He has constantly bestowed upon humanity, even during the long night preceding the birth of Our Lord, when men had but figures and foreshadows with which to appease His wrath and elicit His favors, we are constrained to say that the history of the human race is the history of God's infinite mercy to man. Of this, of course, no true Christian has any doubt, but what we have considered will help us to see that to which we have yet to give thought.

At all times, in all circumstances, no matter whether committed by Jew or Gentile, sin has been so offensive, so great an injury to the majesty of God, as to be infinitely beyond the power of any creature, whether Angel or man, to repair its mischief. It is in this, in fact, that we can comprehend fully the infinite deformity of sin. But in the case of the sins of Catholics, many grave circumstances combine to aggravate their malice, which serve to show that when God bears with a Catholic grossly offending Him, as many alas! do, the expression of His mercy is even much more generous than to Jew or Gentile as such. God's promises, to the very letter, have been verified, and the Catholic is in circumstances, if he will, to enjoy and profit by the rich fruit. He has every provision possible, if he will but take advantage of his happy lot, to enable him to avoid evil and keep what is commanded as his positive duty. Yet, as we know, though he has all possible advantages, and nevertheless falls into, as too many do, sins as black and often as numerous as those of Jew or Gentile, God suffers his insolence, and in some instances with what should seem excessive mercy, and constantly holds out to him the grace to return to His love. Oh, how many most extraordinary instances are recorded of God's mercy to such; and how many there are which are recorded only above! Only by grace from on high can the sinner, like the prodigal of the Scriptures, return to his long-deserted and much-abused

Father—God. How valuable the grace which enables the poor sinner to call a halt in his miserable and ruinous career! It is the gift of a most indulgent Father to a child, to whom He had given full access to all the treasures of grace possible to man on earth, but who for long years most outrageously abused all His love, and added insult to injury to a degree equal to that of those vastly less favored. Without it the unfortunate one's perdition would be inevitable, and long had he conducted himself in a manner sorely calculated to provoke God to abandon him to the awful rigors of His justice. Oh, the patience of God in suffering insults from such tenderly cared-for children every day throughout the world! It reminds one of the sad treatment which God received from His chosen people of old, with the difference that the horrid violence done to Him by Catholics is vastly less excusable. Should it be any wonder to us after this slight view of the abuse of God's mercy by certain so-called Catholics that, at long last some who persist in their wickedness are given over to a reprobate sense, and therefore never receive this most valuable favor—the grace of conversion? Those there are indeed who so abuse God's mercy as to be given over irreparably to their sins in life and in death. This is the most awful misfortune that can befall a human being, and when it is the case of a Catholic, he experiences a forepang of hell till death. On this earth, whilst I speak, God beholds such so-called Catholics. God grant that not one of the kind is in our parish. Who can tell where God's mercy will cease and His justice begin in any particular case? Ah, no one. Can the conversion of one sinner, after long years of sin and daring wickedness, be any guarantee that after the same number of years spent in equal wickedness others will be thus favored? No, indeed; for there are those in hell whilst I speak, who were cut off in the commission of their first mortal sin, and those there are in heaven who spent long years in sin. The reasons for God's movements with men are infinitely just, and rest with Himself. As we see the circumstances, we should be constrained to say that of all others a Catholic is the least deserving of mercy, when, notwithstanding his facilities and advantages, he abandons himself to a life of sin and wickedness. When he sins, and above all when he sleeps in sin, he abuses God's mercy, as is easy to perceive more than any other. The grace of conversion to such a one is all the more an extraordinary expression of God's infinite mercy. To waive the consideration of this grace, which not indeed infrequently has been accorded great sinners, must we not say that they are but the very few who have not at some stage of their lives stood in need of it, and owed thereto their happy transition from death to life? Can we not, therefore, see that as God's mercy has been more generous to Catholics than to others, their sins are a greater abuse of His mercy than those of others, and His tender mercy which follows and conducts them back to His favor is all the more extraordinary? When, therefore, the Apostle pronounces it the duty of the Gentile, having by His mercy been converted to the faith, to glorify God, it is not difficult to see how much greater reason the Catholic, called back from the death of sin, has to glorify God for His mercy. We are greater debtors to God's mercy, in any case, than others, and therefore (I speak of us born and brought up in the faith); we, more than converted

Jew or Gentile, should "glorify God for His mercy."

In conclusion we should remember that it is by a good life that God is glorified for His mercy. This means nothing more nor less for ordinary Christians than to observe the duties of a practical Catholic. The daily prayers must be said, precepts obeyed, and the Sacraments frequented. Whoever is wanting in these is yet insensible of the debt which he owes to God's infinite mercy, and not yet converted. It becomes all to examine themselves to-day, and see if in truth they are daily giving glory to God for His mercy by truly practical Catholic lives.

III.

THIRD SUNDAY OF ADVENT.

"Let your modesty be known to all men: the Lord is nigh." Phil. iv. 5.

People will practice what the Apostle teaches in this text in proportion as they cultivate a tender conscience. According as they advance in this most to be desired of all Christian qualities, will the fear of God and a dread of giving scandal or disedification grow in them. Though the eyes of men be far from them, their conscience will not allow them to forget that the all-seeing eye of God is upon them, nor will it permit them to be ignorant of their Christian obligation to edify others. From all this springs that truly Christian quality which we designate as self-respect, and which all of us so highly admire in man or woman. What the Apostle would teach us in our text must, therefore, to be genuine, be the reflection of a tender conscience.

The best means to make use of to acquire such a conscience is to conquer all shame and false reserve, and be open and honest in confession and confiding in our confessor. We should look upon our spiritual director as the physician of our souls, and as we should value their health, we should conceal from him no lurking malady. We should not act the part of patients who desire to be cured, but through false delicacy refuse to reveal the malady. Nor should we in doubtful matters assume the responsibility of deciding the case for ourselves without submitting it to our director; he (not we) is the divinely appointed judge. It is to be feared that in this most important matter not a few are seriously at fault, and the sad consequence is their consciences become seared and hard. You need no argument to understand the deadening effects which such an abuse must have on the conscience. Of all calamities, a conscience thus abused under the guise of good is decidedly the worst, and is fraught with the greatest danger. Persons possessing such consciences need but the occasion to act without respect to what St. Paul teaches in our text, as is but too well verified. Since around this duty of honestly and frankly opening our conscience to our spiritual director clusters every good for the Christian soul; since this duty well performed is the very soul of a good life, it is easy to perceive the earnest devotion which should attend its every branch. For the thorough discharge of duty at the sacramental point, the foregoing work of examination, should be exact without scrupulosity, and hallowed by fervent prayer. The light from the spirit of God which spreads its rays at the humble and fervent voice of prayer, will enable us to see ourselves with a clearness of vision that we could not otherwise hope to have. This is where the great mistake of those lies who abuse this all-important means of cultivating a tender conscience. They seek not light to discover themselves, nor strength to overcome certain temptations which crowd upon them, to touch upon serious maladies lightly in confession, from the spirit of God in prayer. But we should not forget that besides the light and strength so necessary, there is another indispensable quality to our preliminary work which is undoubtedly the fruit of thoughtful prayer. I refer to the sorrow so necessary which must, to be justifying, be coupled with a resolute will to amend our ways before God and man. This is the very soul of the work of making the right use of this means by excellence of cultivating a tender conscience. Since, then, this is the great means of cultivating tenderness of conscience, it follows that by all those who desire a tender conscience, all Christians certainly should desire such a conscience, it ought to be resorted to with becoming frequency. Every use of it enables them to see themselves more minutely, and set them anew upon their guard. In this way deliberate defects will gradually become less frequent, and the fewer in our daily lives they become, the greater will be the shock to the conscience when one is committed. Supposing, then, that all who aspire to tenderness of conscience are careful to sanctify their daily life with heartfelt prayer, and that every night before retiring they call themselves to an account of how they have spent the day, I will call your attention to another admirable means of cultivating tenderness of conscience. I refer to the matter of good reading, which, alas! is so much neglected by too many Catholics.

We can understand the value of good reading for the purpose we have in view, when we recollect that it fills our minds with the ideas and sentiments of those who were singularly blessed with the boon of a tender conscience. Certainly books written by such people are eminently calculated to aid us in our aspirations. Few can meditate to much advantage unless aided by a good book, furnishing matter every sentiment of which, when duly pondered, comes home to their souls with untold benefit. Yet, as you know, we should think, in other words meditate, to have religion do its blessed work in our souls, and since meditation is so difficult, why not make serious and well-applied reading supply the want? It is a matter very certain that all who are given to good reading are persons of tender consciences who most fully put in practice the admonition of St. Paul: "Let your modesty be known to all men: the Lord is nigh." Good reading is one of the greatest aids to both mental and vocal prayer, and prayer disposes a person to frequently submit himself for grace and guidance to his spiritual director. So you see, one works on the other, and when one is treated with indifference the whole work suffers. I am indeed sorry to have it to say that it is my experience that good religious reading is treated with great indifference by too many Catholic people. How few, generally speaking, are the good books which have a place in many Catholic family homes? and even the few are seldom looked into. Other books, the sentiments of which are not of a kind calculated to cultivate tenderness of conscience, can be found in generous numbers, nor do they want for readers. Is it any wonder, then, that the number in every parish blessed with tender consciences is so small, and that as a consequence the number that really live up to the admonition of St. Paul in our text, is very far from being as large as it should be?

Too much value cannot be set on the blessing of a tender conscience, the outgrowth of which is the duty pointed out to us by the holy Apostle. For, as we considered in the beginning, the man of a tender conscience fears God and dreads scandal or disedification.

Where all these are, will we find without fail, that ever to be admired Christian self-respect. Ah, that Catholics had more of this hallowed attraction!

IV.

FOURTH SUNDAY OF ADVENT.

"Therefore judge not before the time." 1 Cor. iv. 5.

One of the sins into which pride or self-esteem betrays people is to hold court in their own interior, and without witness, or even very often circumstantial evidence, pass sentence upon their neighbor. The super-excellence which they assume as their own prepares them to undervalue others. To such ridiculous extremes are some people carried in this direction that they cannot see a fault in themselves, or a virtue in their neighbor. The voice of reason or conscience their self-esteem silently ignores, and their sentence goes as if they were constituted judges of all but themselves. Have they heard of defection in one of a particular pursuit, then all thus engaged stand condemned. The signs of virtue in others are either the external show of hypocrites, or at least questionable. Consideration for human frailty they never entertain; allowance for peculiarity of disposition they never grant; and for the tempting circumstances of their less fortunate neighbor they have no compassion. To what deliriums, pride forces people; how it deadens conscience to a sense of wrong; how it banishes charity from man!

Those self-constituted judges in their conception of others esteem themselves as mighty clever. At sight they dispose of all that come their way, ere they have any hearing. From one's look or word, they credit him with this vice or that, as their whim suggests. His best actions are attributed to bad motives, or if not bad, at least misleading; his levity is interpreted as but the introduction to sins with which he is not unfamiliar. If humble, they consider him mean-spirited; if meek, they count him a coward; and if submissive and resigned in time of trial, they assign it to heedlessness. In short, rash-judging people cannot without violence to their feelings admit any good in others, or any evil in themselves. Every conversation in their neighbor's favor is not to their taste, and though the evidence of his merit be ever so clear, the most they give is a half-hearted indorsement. Every favor bestowed on him they consider a sign of over-estimation of his merit, and attribute the liberality of the giver to a want of insight which prevented the detection of the deceit of the recipient. Surely this is not a Christian part, and yet, alas! too many Christians act it. Pride, their own self-esteem, so blinds them that only in themselves are they pleased. Is this not a repetition of that spirit of those of old, who, for esteem of themselves refused to see virtue in perfection itself—the model man—Christ Jesus?

In any case such a disposition in a man is deplorable, but when the matter so judged of the neighbor is grave, every rash judgment is damnable. Charity cannot be in the soul where the neighbor is so cruelly treated whilst without opportunity to defend himself. He is judged without trial; he is condemned without proof, and all by those who not only have no right to judge, but are expressly forbidden to do so. "Judge not, says Our Lord, that you may not be judged; for with what judgment you judge, you shall be judged." Can it not be said that instead of exalting themselves, persons addicted to rash judging, who, like other people, speak from the fulness of their hearts, betray the corruption of their own hearts? Do they not show that they are not unfamiliar with those sins which they rashly attribute to others? People who are innocent themselves are not the ones to pass rashly upon others. But those who have corrupt hearts, it would seem, take a delight in attributing a like corruption to others. Like the fool who esteems himself as wise, whilst he counts every one else a fool, they by their sallies upon their neighbor, would fain pass as virtuous. St. Paul forgets not to tell those who are fond of passing rashly upon others that in so doing they but condemn themselves: " Wherefore thou art inexcusable, O man, whoever thou art that judgest; for wherein thou judgest another thou condemnest thyself, for thou dost the same thing which thou judgest." Rom. ii. 1. Our Lord, too, shows very clearly the character of rash judgers, when He tells them they are hypocrites with a beam in their own eye, whilst they would condemn their neighbor for the mote in his: "Thou hypocrite, cast out first the beam out of thy own eye, and then shalt thou see to cast the mote out of thy brother's eye." Matt. vii. 5. In the case of others, such people would have white black, virtue vice, but in their own the black must be white, and vice virtue. How inconsistent pride and its concomitant vices render people, nay, Christian people, who would throw a mask around their corruption and pose as virtuous at the sore expense of others! Beware of the man that is ready in season and out of it, to condemn others. In him, as developments of his pride, can be found envy and hatred, which suggest many of his rash judgments. As the most delicate hues appear blue when seen through spectacles of that color, virtues in others seem vices when eyed by the envious. This precisely was how the Pharisees viewed the most brilliant virtues of Our Lord, and all of us know the woes pronounced against them. Injustice is done the one rashly judged, though it be confined to an interior act; pride is nourished by every such act; hatred increased, and envy fed. But the man who is rash in his judgments, experience teaches, will not be content with the interior act. From the fulness of his heart his mouth will speak slander and then, oh then, what untold mischief ensues!

As you perceive, I have been arguing against all rash judging, but before I close it may be well to remark that I do not consider the case rash or unlawful, when to protect himself, a man from well-founded proofs suspects another, but reserves judgment till he hears the one suspected in his own defense. In this great care should be observed, and no one should allow himself to be carried beyond the weight of the proofs. All of us know that what sometimes appear proofs are only so in imagination, and on close investigation fall flat. Great care should therefore be taken to sound them to their lowest depths, lest a sore injustice be done to the one suspected by summoning him to defend himself. In this, as you must see, one can be guilty of rash judgment and an actually sore mortification for the one accused, by rushing to a conclusion before thoroughly investigating the proofs.

Let us then, dear people, keep ourselves free from this hateful vice of rash judging; let us ever remember that by it we injure our neighbor, nourish corruption in ourselves, and offend God in a variety of ways. Let us always try to see good in our neighbor where evil is not evident, or when the latter prevails, do what we can for his correction. We should always remember that the more thoroughly we judge ourselves, the less inclined will we be to see faults in others.

V.
SUNDAY WITHIN THE OCTAVE OF CHRISTMAS.

"And if a son, an heir also through God."—Gal. iv. 7.

Through the mercy of God, we were raised in holy Baptism, to the exalted dignity of His children and heirs to His heavenly kingdom. How fortunate he is esteemed to be who is the son of an earthly king and heir to his passing kingdom, but alas! how poorly prized by thoughtless Catholics is the sublime honor of being the children of the King of kings, and the most glorious privilege of heirs to His everlasting kingdom! This humiliating contrast of Christians' estimate between temporal and eternal honors and possessions, serves to show how earthly minded, how far even they are from the keen, religious appreciation, it becomes them to have for matters eternal. Want of serious and frequent thought respecting the inestimable value of what God has in store for His faithful servants, is responsible in no slight degree for the fabulous value which to their shame, some Catholics attach to earthly things, and the soul-dooming indifference which they too often betray regarding the vast riches of eternity. If they would not continue in this evil bent of disposition till it shall be too late, it becomes them to learn of God rather than of stupidly erring men, the relative value of temporal and eternal riches. Too long indeed have otherwise well-meaning Christians followed the opinions and examples of men, who have no thought beyond this world, in an error which, alas! covers the face of the earth, and what is most to be deplored, numbers no small fraction of every community as its dupes of those whose Catholic instruction should have the contrary fruit. Most undoubtedly it would have produced good Christian fruit had not the contagion, owing to constant contact with those deeply affected, proved too strong. Should those be here who are victims of the disease of esteeming temporal matters more than eternal, it may prove of great value to them to mature well in their hearts what God's word has on the subject.

Our Lord, in most direct terms, gives us to understand that all else should, if necessary, be forfeited for what is laid up for us in eternity. This He taught not only in word, but also by His blessed example, during thirty and three years. Now, it should seem to any Catholic at least, that His authority on this all-important matter is vastly safer to follow than that of men who have not a thought beyond this world. Yet they can number their followers and imitators by millions, whilst those who follow and learn from Our Lord, in His spirit as well as in the letter of His all holy teaching, are comparatively few. He tells us that "the kingdom of heaven is like unto a treasure hidden in a field, which when a man hath found he hideth, and for joy thereof goeth and selleth all that he hath and buyeth that field." In the full sense of the term, heaven is pre-eminently a treasure, for it lacks absolutely nothing in point of excellence or duration. It is that full, complete treasure for which the human soul, obeying the promptings of her nature, yearns, even though all the rich resources of this world were exhausted to satisfy her cravings. To esteem its superexcellence, so as to count all that this world values in comparison to it as mere dross, is, in the sense of the text, " to find it;" and to renounce in spirit, so as even in the midst of great worldly riches, to be unattached to all, save this treasure above, is "to sell all to purchase" the object of our soul's yearnings. Again, Our Lord calls the kingdom of heaven a pearl of so great value that one should not hesitate to deem whatever else he may have as merely a means to purchase it. "The kingdom of heaven is like to a merchant seeking good pearls; who when he had found one pearl of great price, went his way and sold all that he had, and bought it." Matt. xii. Is not this teaching of Our Lord a most direct contradiction to the materialistic tendency of the age, which sets scarcely any value on eternal riches, whilst the false goods of this world are stupidly valued as if all-sufficient and everlasting? Are there not in this congregation persons who have been, unfortunately for them, actuated with this erroneous spirit of the age to a degree that would be an occasion of surprise when detected even in pagans? "Blessed are those servants," says Our Saviour, " whom the Lord, when He cometh, shall find watching." Can it be said that Catholics, who not unlike their pagan neighbors, idolize the goods of this world, and practically seem to set little or no value upon their inheritance as children of God, are embraced among those upon whom this benediction is pronounced? Are they watching, in the sense of Our Lord, for the treasure, the pearl of their inheritance? If they are, then verily all the saintly men and women of every age, who have followed in spirit and to the letter the blessed example and teaching of Our Lord, have made a grand mistake. Watch!—no one will deny the worshippers of this world do, aye, and if they watched half so well for their everlasting inheritance, its possession would indeed be the reward of their vigilance. But no, their glory seems to be in present material success; this is their coveted treasure, their pearl of great value, for which they hesitate not to forego even their eternal inheritance. God grant they may discover their mistake, and profit by the discovery before it will be too late!

When the rebel angels had forfeited their everlasting inheritance, God in His goodness created another race of intelligent, free beings, though less perfect in nature, to enjoy what the former had by pride forever lost. We are of that race, and when the number of the elect of our race shall be completed, then will come the end of time. Think then of the inestimable value of our eternal inheritance, when God has deemed it worthy of Him, to enable us to enjoy it, to exercise in ways most extraordinary His Almighty power and sovereign dominion. Behold the wonderful works of God above, beneath, and around us, for, in all of them are we reminded of the inconceivable value of the eternal riches to which we are heirs. Since God has so generously favored us, good, bad, and indifferent as we are in this world, with means to make our tarry here even agreeable, and with every requisite to attain our inheritance hereafter, should not His present expression of goodness towards us serve as an earnest of the wonderous, the immense riches to which we are heirs, and enable us to religiously appreciate the words of St. Paul? "Neither eye hath seen, nor ear heard, nor heart of man conceived what God hath prepared for them that love Him." All which we see, as well as all that we do not behold as manifestations of His Providence and dominion in governing nature, have next to His accidental glory, the convenience of man as the reason of their existence. Hence for man they exist, and through him who only of all beings on earth can appreciate them, they are occasions of glory to the Creator. But the reason for man's existence is immediately in God Himself, to Whom in the enjoyment of the bliss of heaven he will be forever an occasion of accidental glory. Though man even forfeit his everlasting inheritance by sin and insult, not the less will he be the occasion of accidental glory to God, since he was created for heaven, but by his own perverse will lost his birthright. All, all then of the works of Providence on earth in relation to man, whether visible or invisible, should impress us with the inconceivable value of our inheritance as children of God. But when we raise our thoughts above this world, and contemplate that not only material nature has God employed to enable man to reach his inheritance, but those sublime spirits, the Angels, who deem themselves honored in such an important mission, we should hang our heads in shame at having in the past betrayed so much indifference regarding our title as heirs. And what, after all, do all the foregoing arguments amount to when compared with the one we have yet to think on, as a means to give us the highest possible conception of the vastness of the riches to which we are heirs? We lost them, and to buy them back, no less a price could possibly suffice than the sufferings and merits and death of Our Lord and Saviour Jesus Christ. The price given has been infinite; can we, therefore, any longer value aught else than our everlasting inheritance above, for which Christ Jesus paid an infinite price?

VI.
FIRST SUNDAY AFTER EPIPHANY.

"And be not conformed to this world."—Romans xii. 2.

The world to which, on the peril of our salvation, the Apostle warns us not to conform, is many sided. It has its atheists, who in public harangues and nefarious literature, ridicule all that is most sacred. Do they speak and write to be heard and read only by their followers? Ah, no! Were they confined to their followers for hearers and readers, religion could be saved the trouble of mourning over the sad effects of their accursed work. To speak in general, who but Christians, who flock to hear them and devour their writings, are responsible for their work? Ah, that we could say that Catholics at least adhere, in an instance like this, to the apostolic warning, by shrinking with horror from either branch of this twofold encouragement, held out to these blasphemous scoffers by so-called Christians. This we cannot say in the face of history, which confronts us with facts that show that certain well-known atheists have flourished in the heart of Catholic nations. Besides, our experience will not allow us to doubt that, in almost every parish, Catholics could be found who hesitate not to listen to such traducers, and introduce their writings into their homes. Is it manly; is it Christian for a man to listen to the vilifier of his father and mother? O Catholic man! Is God not your Father; is the Church not your Mother? How then can you brook with pleasure the insults offered them by the blasphemous lips and accursed writings of such immoral monsters? Who has your best interest the more at heart,—these wretches who would, if they could, destroy every principle of morality, and turn people against whatever is high, holy, and replete with consolation for the human heart; or the priest, who is prepared to give his life for your soul's salvation? The latter you are constrained to admit, for unless you have lost all sense of religion, you must brand them as most dangerous enemies, and honor the priest as the best friend of humanity. Hear, then, his voice, for he but repeats the sentiments of St. Paul, when he says, conform not to the ways of the so-called Christians, who encourage these infamous vilifiers of everything Christian, and of the divine Author of Christianity—Christ.

The world, too, has its legions of Christian posers, who may or may not have entered the door to the Christian ranks, but be that as it may, they shut out God from their ways. Unscrupulous, as might be expected, they are the fruitful agents to lines of conduct to which no good Christian could conform. Wherever they are, there, too, is corruption in one shape or another. From their ranks the country is infested with usurers, bribe-givers and bribe-takers, tricksters of every grade, monopolists, who snatch the morsel of bread from the famishing child, and all those selfish, grasping beings that tend to blotch the fair name of a people. But the mischief is they pass as smart, as very models in our progressive age, and their ways are copied. Too often, indeed, do Catholics drop from the ranks of the practical to those of the nominal, because, forsooth, they have conformed to the line of conduct of those who it is clear give God no place. Almost of a caste with them are those patrons of the fashionable side of the world, who have no regard for modesty when there is a question of fashion. This, too, is true of the pleasure-seeking side, filled by those who never stop to think what is, or is not in conformity with God's law. Whilst places of becoming amusement are of great public utility, it cannot be denied that places of pagan-like sensuous amusements are formidable occasions of moral corruption. To-day this is to an alarming extent true of theatres. How much better the morals of society would be if flesh and blood were not played upon by the suggestive, tempting allurements of the theatre!

But not to prolong the enumeration too far, we will content ourselves with one more side of the world to which, in the words of the Apostle, we must not conform. On it we find persons who protest that their faith, in all the truths of Christianity, is as entire and sound as it should be, yet the tenor of their lives show that they pay but little or no heed to the words of Christ: "What will it profit a man to gain the whole world if he lose his soul." They live as if the affairs of the world should have first place, and salvation a very inferior second, or none at all. How common such people are in almost every Catholic community! Is their manner of life worthy of imitation? Either Christ or they are right. Christ tells us that nothing is comparable in importance to the salvation of our souls. Then a gross mistake are these people guilty of who treat the business salvation as if it were the least important of all the concerns of a man's life. Have we not such people in this parish? Who can perceive the anxiety betrayed by some for the things of this world, and take cognizance of their deplorable indifference in respect to the means of salvation, and pronounce them free from this soul-dooming mistake? Though Catholics, the tenor of their lives does not seem to differ, in so far as making idols of their worldly concerns, from the lives of those neighbors who make no profession whatever of religion. It is true for unworthy motives, such as to avoid criticism, or peradventure to gain and preserve patronage in their business, rather than from obedience to the voice of conscience, they at times show some exterior signs of practical religion. But the idol of their hearts is not disturbed; he holds on as tenaciously as he does to the heart of the non-religious neighbor. Whilst the non-religious in this particular instance seems consistent, the Catholic evinces the other extreme. On earth there does not breathe a more inconsistent being than the instructed Catholic, who is no less a slave to the world than his non-religious neighbor. His life is in such woful contrast with his profession and name as to fill any thinking person with the most gloomy, most rueful forebodings of his eternal interests.

Thus we have but a partial view of the world to which the Apostle refers. And from this imperfect glance, should it not seem to any reasonable person that, to conform to the world, and be a truly practical Christian, must be rated among the impossibilities. Hence, either God or the world must be the all engrossing object of man's heart. God will not, as He tells us, have a divided heart; He must have the whole heart or none. But can a man give God his entire heart and be true to his calling in the world? God, Who demands of man his whole heart, also exacts of him a consistent fidelity to the duties of his station. This is sufficient proof in the matter, but should we desire a variety of testimony, we have but to look to the thrones in heaven, and behold saints from every station in life, who, when on earth were not wanting in a becoming fidelity to their worldly duties, though God was the all engrossing object of their hearts. Tell me, O Catholic man! who conforms to that world against which St. Paul sends out to you on the lips of the priest his word of warning, are you not on the same road with that group of godless mortals, who for things natural have forfeited all sense of eternal truths? Your aim is no higher than theirs, notwithstanding the vast superiority of your advantage. Sound your heart, I beg of you, before it will be too late, and ask yourself in all candor, whether in journeying to eternity on the broad road with such a crowd, you are conformable to right reason, faith, and your own best interests. Should it not occur to you that the way traced out by our blessed Lord, and followed by all the good Christian men and women who are now experiencing the joys of God's "house of many mansions," is most decidedly the one for you? This most safe and most hallowed way is pointed out in these words of Our Lord: "He that doth the will of my Father, he shall enter into the kingdom of heaven."

VII.

SECOND SUNDAY AFTER EPIPHANY.

TRUE FERVOR.

"Be fervent in Spirit."—Romans xii. 2.

True fervor is the acme of devotion. In vain would we expect to find it in persons who are impelled by motives of self-love. When self-love, of a kind with what any animal has for itself, is all that a man possesses, though he may pass as a saint, he has no true Christian fervor. The love which the truly fervent entertain for themselves is a love of charity. The difference is this, the latter begins and centres in God, the former begins and centres in self. By the truly fervent, God is loved for His own sake, and all else only so far as it is harmonious with the love of God. Their wills, though in no way constrained, act under the sweet influence of their love for God. Hence their thoughts, desires, words, and actions are seasoned and regulated by the divine flame which burns in their souls. The duties of their respective stations in life receive so much and no more of their attention as is consistent with this flame of divine love. When God's love says: that and more, their work is not yet done; when His love says: that and no more, the limit for them is reached. In all circumstances beyond their control they see the Divine will, and bow in humble submission, rejoicing for what they deem favors direct from God. Here, they say in their hearts, is an occasion to atone for past sins, or, now another interval has arrived, rich in divine favors, of which God sees the need. All for God is the motto of their lives, for they perceive it leads to true greatness, which is the possession and enjoyment of heaven forever. Should it ever occur to them in imitation of the Divine Model of Gethsemane to sue for a lighter measure of His justice, their prayer is never without the hallowed ending: "Thy will, not mine be done." Thus we see the surpassing value of that fervor of spirit which the Apostle exhorts us to have. Who that desires to reach the ultimate end of his existence perceives not that he should be its possessor? Motives are numerous urging us to its acquirement. Let us give them thought. But ere we do so we should remember that true fervor consists in a strict fidelity to God's will expressed in the Commandments and the precepts of the Church.

We are the results of the creative act of God, and His power of creating is only used for a purpose worthy of Himself. Therefore we are upon this earth for a purpose—a purpose worthy of God. Time and eternity are within its compass. If we serve the purpose in time we are certain to do so in eternity. "This visible world is made only for one that is invisible, and the Lord of all things disposes and regulates all that passes in the one, only as a foundation on which to establish the other for the sake of the elect, that they may obtain the salvation which is in Christ Jesus unto heavenly glory." Thus we see, to attain the end of our existence in eternity, we must serve the end for which we have it in time. "If thou wilt enter into life, keep the Commandments." Who could reasonably dispute a watchmaker's right to make the watch, the work of his hands, serve his legitimate purpose? Is God therefore doing an injustice to man when, leaving him in the enjoyment of his freedom, He demands him to serve the purpose for which He created him? Is He not the absolute Sovereign of His creatures? What mortal, then, has a right to question or dispute His authority? No reasonable person will question the right of earthly sovereigns in the legitimate exercise of their authority. On the contrary, all loyal subjects and law-loving people will strive to maintain their authority. So for infinitely superior reasons should we act in respect to God. We should maintain a strict fidelity in ourselves to God's holy will expressed in the Commandments, and the precepts of the Church. We should do more; we should do whatever our circumstances would permit to promote respect for God's authority in others. This is true fervor. How can we look upon all those gifts of which we are the possessors, that have stamped upon them the sacred impress of God's divine goodness, and withhold fidelity to His blessed will? Our life, our preservation, our powers, our talents, our lights, gifts, and graces are all the blessed effects of His goodness, for which eternity is too short in which to thank Him. A good mother's love for the child of her bosom is the most tender, is the most strong to be found among mortals. But what parity is there between it and that infinite love which God entertains for each of us; what comparison is there between its humble effects and the blessed effects of God's love extended to all of us? "Can a mother forget her infant so as not to have pity on the son of her womb? And if she should forget, yet I will not forget thee." God is infinitely superior to His creatures, and His love is infinitely greater than the most complete of which they are capable. The effects of His love which the most favored, because the most worthy, experience in this life, are to those He has reserved for them in the next life but what the glimpse of Thabor was to the glory in the great hereafter, which He had reserved for the Apostles who were in ectasies over what they saw at the Transfiguration. Had we no other motive but gratitude, it would seem that it should be all-sufficient to urge us to show fervor of spirit in fidelity to His will expressed in the Commandments and the precepts of His Church. The thunders and lightnings of Sinai, amid which He communicated His written law to man, were significant of what should be the consequences of their violation. Every detail of God's law is most important in the estimation of the truly fervent. How far, therefore, are the great majority of Christians from true fervor! When we take the trouble to compare the ways of the world with the letter and the spirit of God's law, and the precepts of His Church, how easily the sentence glides into our minds: " Many are called, but few are chosen "? And yet those whose lives are at such variance with His will thus expressed have the same means held out to them which enable the comparative few to be truly fervent. The majority take little or no notice of them, but the few lay hold of them with hearty good will, and in consequence they are carried forward by divine grace which they acquire by their proper use. Whatever may be their circumstances, it must be conceded that they are serious and correct thinkers on the only business which is exclusively personal. All others are spending themselves in pursuits which will benefit others rather than themselves, and neglecting that which is purely their own personal business. More thought on the motives is what is sadly needed to excite fervor in those who have none. Who is better rewarded for their trouble than the truly fervent? They have peace here, and they will have the peace and joys of God's elect hereafter. But all others are deplorably barren of peace here, and preparing to weep throughout eternity. Let us, dear people, seriously pass upon this matter, and see how we stand. Are we unfortunately in line with the thoughtless majority, or fortunately proceeding with the thoughtful and fervent? Let the conscience of each give the answer. If we find ourselves devoid of the spirit of fervor which manifests itself in fidelity to the law of God, we should remember that the advice of the Apostle is far safer to follow than the voice of those whom we have followed up to this. He tells us to be fervent in spirit, which means to observe the law, and Our Lord tells us that the keeping of the law is the only condition on which we can enter into life eternal.

VIII.

THIRD SUNDAY AFTER EPIPHANY.

KINDNESS AND ITS EFFECTS.

"If it be possible as much as is in you, have peace with all men."
—Romans xii. 18.

It is unquestionably true that kindly-disposed persons with good, religious hearts, always when occasions present themselves, prove a success in effecting much good in others. Their society is generally esteemed most agreeable by the well-meaning; their advices and corrections in the interest of the erring are tempered with a judicious and becoming deference for their feelings, and their example is a source of edification and deemed well worthy of imitation. Whilst some are by nature more inclined to kindness than others, real Christian kindness comes within the compass of charity, and is therefore much more the effect of grace than of nature in our best models. In fact most of those who have distinguished themselves in the Christian sense of its practise were by nature quite the opposite to kind. Their names have been recorded in the hearts of the people among whom they lived, or on historic pages, as those of the meekest and kindest of men, and for the distinction they have been indebted to the divine unction of grace, which carried them to their respective degrees of perfection in their imitation of the Divine model. Kindness, like all other moral gifts, is within the power of all to attain. All wilful unkindnesses, therefore, are one's own fault, and by consequence sinful. No one conversant with the duties of his obligation of charity towards his neighbor need be informed that respect for the feelings of others is one of them. Our neighbor's temper is his own affair, for which we are in no way responsible, but we will be held accountable for all wilful and uncalled-for breaches of his peace by our unkindness. Peculiarity of disposition is as numerous as individuals. To avoid mistakes, therefore, the man of true Christian kindness will observe precaution till his acquaintance is fully ripe. People we meet who have such peculiar imaginations as make it a matter of grave difficulty for them to see things in any other light than their own; others we come in contact with, who are members of some party or organization, the interest and reputation of which depend largely on certain erroneous ideas, with which all the members are imbued; and large, indeed, is the number of those who hold to opinions and views which have the prepossession for them of being those in which they were brought up, but all the same are largely at variance with truth. Now, how to carry ourselves amid so great a variety, and stand for the truth on all occasions, with the charitable view of benefiting all, without offence to any, is peculiarly the work of those whom religion makes kind. None but the kindly-disposed will succeed in having truth supersede error, and should they fall short of success, they will, at least, have the consolation of not having given offence. Besides those to whom we have referred, we will not fail to find the number large of persons who, because of certain advantages imaginary or real, are quite positive and stiff in their opinions. Whilst the man with true Christian kindness would not be so unfair as to assume this weakness without positive evidence, of any one in particular, yet his manner of acting among all in general will prudently be as if it were a common proclivity. Such precaution cannot possibly do harm, but, on the contrary, prepares the way for their esteem which, when once gained, he is sure at least of a respectful hearing. He speaks in the very delicate circumstances, after mature conviction, that he is equal to the occasion, and only when duty or charity constrains him to do so with a view to good. The harsh manner of some, which gives the impression that their aim is to pain, rather than set right, can never be laid to his charge. He scrupulously guards against all manner of gall or bitterness, and skilfully seasons and sweetens what he says to a degree that robs it of all sting, and conveys the impression that he is prompted, as he really is, by motives of kindness. A real Christian gentleman, he betrays nothing of a domineering self-conceit or of an inclination to undervalue, but on all occasions carries himself with great deference for the feelings of persons entertaining opinions different from his. Never does he allow heat or passion to betray him into the very great fault of wounding his neighbor's feelings, or marring the beauty of the truth which he announces. Truth coming from his lips, appears in its full lustre and beauty, and is therefore rendered attractive to those who might otherwise never stop to give it consideration. It is a great mistake which some are guilty of to imagine that civil and gentlemanly manners are only a gloss to set people off, and not in truth a part of our Christian duty. Slow to take and slow to give offence ought to be our rule, and the further we keep from aught offensive, the more strictly do we adhere to this rule. There is a wide difference between the manners of the empty fop and those of the Christian gentleman, but with a view, as is sometimes the case, to avoid the former, to commit faults against the latter, is reprehensible. What state would society be in were it robbed of civility and good manners? And to whom should we look for correct civility of manners, if not to the man whom religion has refined? We are in some way or other depending on each other; Providence seems to have so circumstanced us that union and peace might prevail among us. Whatever, therefore, contributes to peace among us, meets the approbation of His good pleasure. This is true of kindness or civility of manners.

Religion is the theme of many disputes which are attended with no good results, but may be safely designated as so many breaches of peace among men. Catholics there are who seem to have a strong inclination to be champions of faith, and in their discussions truth is made to suffer, they being wanting in qualifications for the duty they assume. It would be much better for the cause of truth, for others, and for themselves, were they to comply with what is required of them, which is to leave this delicate matter to persons qualified to attend to it, and content themselves with aiding in the conversion of others, by fervent prayer and exemplary lives. Even persons well qualified for the delicate circumstances must be careful that the result will justify their undertaking. There are persons who, to express it in the words of Our Lord: " hate the light," and to strive to open their eyes by the force of argument and reason is, it would seem, to have them shut them the closer. It would be idle, nay, more, it might be sinful, no matter how well qualified we may be, to enter into religious discussions with such people. The man of true Christian kindness who is always a man of peace will never expose the cause of truth and of peace by such an imprudent venture. But when the prospect is without clouds, that a conversation can be conducted amicably, and with good fruit to his neighbor, he is never slow to present the truth in the most telling manner and in its most attractive garb. This is the secret of the great success of some who effect so much good in others. They not only live in peace with their fellow-man, but they would gladly lead him to peace with God. Peacemakers indeed are they of whom Our Lord said: "Blessed are the peacemakers for they shall be called the children of God."

In conclusion we should remember that if peace be wanting among those who have not yet come under the saving refinement of religion, there is no excuse whatever to justify its want among us. Our religion teaches us not only how we should preserve peace among ourselves, but likewise how we should conduct ourselves, so as to preserve it with those who, unfortunately for themselves, do not worship God in truth. When it teaches us to have charity for all, it teaches us to be kind to all without exception, for one of the duties of charity is kindness. By observing it on all occasions in communicating with our fellow-man, we will not only obey the voice of the Apostle: "have peace with all men," but we may be the occasion of leading many poor benighted souls to peace with God, and thus merit the benediction which Our Lord pronounced on peacemakers.

IX.

SEPTUAGESIMA SUNDAY.

"I therefore so run, not as at an uncertainty; I so fight, not as one beating the air."—I. Cor. ix. 26.

The lessons of this text are in marked contrast with the half-hearted way in which many Christians exert themselves, and fight their spiritual enemies for God's eternal prize. The prize for which St. Paul and all the true followers of Our Lord have run and fought, is the same as that for which to run and fight we entered the Christian ranks. Though while in this world " we know not whether we are worthy of love or hatred;" that is to say, absolutely; we are, however, aware of the conditions on which love will take the place of hatred; and we can have a moral certainty, which is all sufficient, concerning their fulfilment. Can each one here with hand on heart in the presence of his God, say that were he at this moment to cross the threshold of eternity, he would obtain the prize because he is morally certain that he fulfilled the conditions which, if his case required it, forced hatred to give place to love? If so, then each of us can say with St. Paul: " I therefore so run, not as at an uncertainty." But it is unfortunately true that only the very few, when taken to task, can thus speak on what centres all the importance of a man's existence. Do they tarry in such uncertainty concerning the corruptible prizes held out to them by the world? Ah, no!

Whilst there is question of uncertainty respecting them, anxiety rests heavily upon them, and their best energies are set in motion till the warrant of their success is in sight. They run and fight so as to obtain the world's perishable prizes, whilst they allow God's immortal prize to go by default. This is the general tenor of the ways of, alas! too many in every parish.

Why is it that people are so ill-concerned regarding the crown or ruin of their existence? It is because they stop not to think seriously of the superexcellence of the one, and the soul-dooming awfulness of the other. The fault is their own, for God affords them ample opportunity to exercise their minds and hearts on these truths. Lost opportunities furnish, perhaps, the most bitter ingredient of the remorse of those now in hell. It is to be feared that many who are now living and passing as Catholics will, too, weep eternally for lost opportunities. Because, failing to utilize them, they have sunk into "ungodliness," and become the prey of "worldly desires." Though they preserve a semblance of religion they have, contrary to law and conscience, torn their hearts from God, and prostituted them to desires that were once fashionable with those who are now in hell. Practically they are not in the race and fight for the prize, which is the eternal, predestined crown of human existence. Their consciences upbraid them with the crime of the destruction in themselves of the principle of spiritual life, which is the love of God above all else. God's service is devoid of attractions for them; they have no taste—they have for it a cold aversion. Detail after detail of it is to them the occasion of pain and loathing. Their self-love cannot brook even for God and His prize aught that would count against their satisfaction, ease, or convenience. In a word, they are cold and insensible to God and His eternal prize, and all thoughts of virtue and piety fill them with disgust and aversion. This is their case in the face of Our Lord telling them that only by religious violence can they obtain the prize: "The kingdom of heaven suffers violence, and the violent bear it away;" this is their case in the face of St. Paul telling them that they must "run and fight with the certainty" within their power, to procure the prize; this is their case whilst every maxim of the Gospel announces to them that on the penalty of damnation they must mortify, deny, and penance themselves. In their daily lives they put God's prize last of all as a matter of importance; and whilst in all else they will have certainty, they seem content to let this hang on an uncertainty suggestive of their utter eternal ruin. Should a man neglect to make certain his material interests, they are among the first to pronounce him foolish, and single him out as an object of criticism; but their own profoundly stupid and perilous negligence, concerning their eternal interests, they never seem to once realize. Like persons blind rushing towards a precipice they, spiritually blind, rush, contenting themselves with a slim, heartless display of religion, towards the eternal precipice of God's justice. The loss of the great prize and the terrible alternative, which stare them from a no distant future, pass with them as if fiction. Should any one impede the progress of their material interest, at once they lay hold of the arms of defence. They fight not "as one beating the air," but as men intent on victory. No circumstance must be omitted; no discipline is considered too severe; no inconvenience is thought of when their material interests are at stake. They study; they are wise according to the world; they never tire working with brain and brawn; and all for no higher motives than to carry away the prizes held out to them by the world. Whilst they thus run and fight for prizes from which, at least in death, they must be torn, their spiritual enemies have no great difficulty in causing them to lose sight of the prize which, when once gained, can never be lost. They treat it as if its value did not warrant sufficient for which to run and fight, though they are as absolutely certain of its eternal, pre-eminent value, as they are of their own existence, and as absolutely certain as that they must die; that to obtain it they must both run and fight, as the millions before them who now enjoy it have done.

In conclusion we should remember that, as this is Septuagesima Sunday, we are within the shadow of the Sacred Season, which proved the turning point of the lives of many who are now in heaven. Should there be those here who find that what we have considered is a true outline of their lives in the past, all that is most dear to them proclaims the necessity of a change. What better time could they select to effect it than the present, which is an introduction to that season so rich in divine favors for all those in a state that renders them worthy recipients? An opportunity so propitious may never again dawn upon them. Up to the present they have been foolishly taking chances on a matter of the gravest importance—their lot in eternity. Act not, I beg of you, any longer the foolhardy part in a matter which means your eternal crown or ruin, and in which those who are now in hell have figured to their ruin before you. Like them you have not, up to the present, been running and fighting to avoid the ruin, and gain the crown of your existence; but like children you have contented yourselves in running and fighting for the world's gilded trinkets. Now at least you should begin with St. Paul to run with certainty and fight effectually, so as to avoid the ruin, and gain the crown of your existence. "I therefore so run, not as at an uncertainty: I so fight, not as one beating the air."

X.

SEXAGESIMA SUNDAY.

"Who is scandalized, and I am not on fire."—II. Cor. xi. 29.

Thus spoke the priest in the Apostolic age, and thus might the priest speak to-day. Perhaps in the calendar of vice there is not one, the mere thought of which so fires with zeal to counteract its ruinous effects, the priest in charge of souls, as scandal. From the depths of his soul he deplores it as a cancer in the breast of society, and dreads it because of the terrible havoc which follows in its wake. Both directly and indirectly his voice is constantly raised against the iniquity of the givers and takers of scandal. To-day our text demands for it direct consideration.

Who that ever heard and gave serious thought to the woes pronounced by Our Lord against the scandal-giver, could dare lend himself to such a vice? If the blood of our fellow-man's body cries to Heaven for vengeance to come upon the slayer, the voice of the dying soul that has been murdered by the scandal-giver must thunder at God's throne for the shafts of His justice to strike her slayer. The woes pronounced by Our Lord will not allow us to doubt that her voice will be heard and answerd in the full measure of God's avenging justice. "Wo to the world on account of scandals, for it must needs be that scandal come; but nevertheless wo to that man by whom the scandal cometh." The self-inflicted ignorance of their own weakness and of their need of God's grace, of some, and the consummate malice of others, constrained Our Lord to say: "that scandals must needs come." Weakness and malice among men have therefore infested the world with scandals. The daily and weekly organs literally teem with accounts of them; the stage voices their sentiments, and acts their almost every detail after the most suggestive fashion in the full glare of public view; and books are sent broadcast to perpetuate their memory and universalize their iniquity by the destruction of the greatest possible number of souls. How just then are the words of Our Lord: "Woe to the world on account of scandals!" The terrific wails of dying souls are constantly going up to Heaven calling for its vengeance upon this world of scandal. How much each scandal-giver should fear this vengeance can be understood from these words: "He that shall scandalize one of these little ones that believe in Me, it were better for him that a mill-stone were hanged about his neck, and that he were drowned in the depth of the sea." The world is rank with scandal-givers, nor have wars, nor famines, nor contagions killed more bodies than they have souls. Since the inhabitants of heaven experience so much joy over the conversion of one sinner, could they weep, heaven would be constantly flooded with their tears over the ruin of souls daily murdered by scandal-givers. God's designs in creating those souls for heaven scandal-givers mock, Christ's blood shed for their redemption they trample under foot, and the Holy Ghost's temples they usurp and hand over to the devil, whose agents they are.

Nay, they are even more than his agents, as Our Lord informs us when He says to them: "You are of your father, the devil, and the desires of your father you will do; he was a murderer from the beginning." He murdered the soul of Eve, and whilst content with him for a father, she in turn murdered the soul of Adam, and in her iniquity became the mother of scandal-givers. Who but God can tell where the murderous act or word of the scandal-giver will end its wicked career?

Like the contagion of the body this contagion of the soul flies from one to another. Like the ball let go from on high by the aeronaut, increasing its velocity the farther it travels, scandal acquires new force as it passes down the ages from generation to generation. One first scandalized his neighbor by his profanity. Oh, how the scandal which he gave has travelled; how universal it has become; how many souls it has eternally ruined! Another first scandalized a community by figuring in the divorce court. Behold to what proportions that individual's scandal has grown; what a curse to families, morals, and country it has become! Thus it has been with the other vices so much to be deplored, all of them have had their first abettors, who like Eve did the devil's work in teaching them to others. O man! take a retrospect of the past; view the circumstances of your lapse into your first sin. Were you not the victim of this contagion, and did you not communicate the dread disease to at least another? Thus far you can go, to your own knowledge, and you can easily surmise that your pupil has not been without his. So it is that the nefarious work of the scandal-giver continues long after his body has gone down into the grave, and his soul has passed the judgment-seat of a just God Who "renders to every one according to his works." "Wo to that man by whom scandal cometh."

Difficult indeed is it to imagine how persons responsible for children and domestics, can seriously think on the diabolical nature of scandal-giving, and the woes pronounced against it by Our Lord, and still continue to be rocks of scandal in the heart of their own families. They are such as often as they show themselves indifferent to the sacred duties of religion; they are nothing short of it when their language and actions are unchristian, or as often as they tolerate the like in their children or domestics. O cruel parents! who thus prostitute your vocation; if the woes of scandal-givers will be great, and we have God's word for it that they will, your deserts will demand the ultimate vengeance of an injured God towards His most ungrateful creatures. You will curse the day that you assumed the responsibility to bring up children and govern domestics, not for God, but for His enemy. O self-respecting young man! virtuous maidens! who have God's religion in your hearts, and express it in your lives, forget not that your good name and virtuous bearing have put you in marked contrast with those who have become the slaves of passion. They envy you, and would gladly have you like themselves. Guard yourselves, for those agents of the devil are in wait for you. Be not deluded by their looks; suspect the sincerity of their smooth words and capricious ways. Let it be the rule of your lives to keep aloof from society without tried regard for religion, because the atmosphere is unhealthy. It is better to have a good name, a virtuous life, a peaceful conscience here, and heaven hereafter, than all the friends, and all the influence, and all the riches that could be at the command of man.

In this cursory view, who does not see sufficient to convince him of the malignity of scandal and its ruinous effects? Should it not be the grief of our life if we have ever been the occasion of serious scandal to even one? Where that will end, we know not. Our prayers should constantly go up for that one, and for those to whom he in turn may have communicated the dread contagion; and our lives should be henceforth so edifying as to counteract, as far as possible, the work of the scandal-givers of the community. Though we never can hope to fully repair the injury which we have unfortunately done, in this way we will effect all that is left for us to do. For the rest we must trust to God to forgive us the injury which we have done Him, which we would gladly repair if we could—the impossible He does not exact.

XI.

QUINQUAGESIMA SUNDAY.

"And now there remain, Faith, Hope, Charity, these three; but the greater of these is Charity."—1 Cor. xiii. 13.

All of us, be the divergence of our aims ever so great, are in quest of happiness. But it has only one centre where it can be found, and sad to say, the aims of the vast majority are not directed thither. Long ago has the world been informed by the All Truthful that, to be happy, the human soul must be in possession of unlimited Good. The joy arising from this possession is genuine happiness, but there is only one unlimited Good—God, therefore the possession of God by love is true happiness.

Waiving all consideration of the vast number who make no aim whatever at loving God, are there not, sad to say, those who solemnly professed to love Him and are very far from practising what they professed? Are there not people in this congregation who have been guilty of thus making a blank of their profession? And yet they know on His own solemn word that if they love Him not in this life they will be denied the sublime privilege of doing so in the next; that if they enjoy not, in time, the happiness of possessing Him by grace, they will not, in eternity, experience the delight of possessing Him in glory. Can the Catholic who is living in a state of fluctuation between grace and sin, claim that he fulfils the great precept of loving God?

Can he who remains one month out of twelve in a state of grace, make the claim? Is God really loved by people, and oh, how numerous they are! who, for their own satisfaction, honor, or interest, hesitate not to violate His commandments and the precepts of His Church? Where is the habitual; where is the intimate love of Thee, O God! in such people; and yet, great God! they are no small proportion of the people of every parish who made solemn profession of loving Thee. Not unfrequently do such people express great surprise that they feel so miserably unhappy. Their lively imaginations or their peculiar tenderness of nature, coupled with some perfunctory prayers, pronounced without heart or sincerity, may have some time in the past wrought them up into illusory sentiments which they falsely deemed love, and now their wonder is that such loving souls as they are should so experience the misery of unhappiness. Sensible sentiments, even when true, have nothing whatever to do with the love of God in the soul; they are favors of God which He confers when and on whom He pleases. They are never, however, bestowed save on those who really love God. Besides, "Not all who will say Lord, Lord, shall enter the kingdom of heaven," but every one who will have shown his love for God by keeping His commandments, shall enter:—"If you love Me, keep My commandments." This demanded test they are unable to point to, thus betraying that they have not really loved God, their heartless prayers and illusory sentiments being nothing to the purpose. The man who really loves God has the harmony of a voice from within, which makes him certain, because it is produced by the love of God in his soul. That is the voice of conscience, which is without harmony so long as God is not loved, in the observance of His commandments and the precepts of His Church. When these are the habitual rules of a man's life, which no consideration could induce him to knowingly and willingly violate, then the voice of his conscience has its true Christian ring, and happiness as far as it can be experienced in this exile, is his assured portion. This has been the blessed portion of the saintly men and women of every age who have been the glory of the Church, because their sentiments have been like unto those of St. Paul: "For I am sure that neither death, nor life, nor angels, nor principalities, nor powers, nor things present, nor things to come, nor might, nor height, nor depth, nor any other creature shall be able to separate us from the love of God, which is in Christ Jesus, Our Lord."

When with the eyes of faith we look up to heaven and behold God, "as through a glass darkly and in part," in all the infinite glory of His Godhead, and then look out upon the universe, the vast production of His one word, and from nothing, should we not justly account ourselves infinitely favored beings, to be allowed to love Him? Is it not a violence to our nature to prevent our hearts from loving an all-lovable, an infinitely lovable object?—Such is God. But when we look in upon ourselves and read upon everything save our sins, which we call ours, that true inscription, "the gift of God's goodness," how, without violence to every instinct of our better nature, can we refrain from loving Him? To be really true to ourselves, and to fully answer the ends of our vocation, both here and in the great hereafter, we must love Him as He demands. Without the love of his God there is no happiness for man in this life, nor in the next; nay, the most dire misery awaits him both here and in eternity. Still more; God has given us a command to love Him, and that too, under the awful penalty of everlasting wo, to all who will persist in violating it till the end of their career on earth. Is it not then clear that our existence, our life, our eternity, if we love not God, will prove so many curses to us, instead of rich blessings which He, the Giver, intended they should be?

Now, dear people, you who cannot say, when you compare your lives with the commandments, with an honest conscience, that you love God, why do you complain of your unhappiness? Do you not perceive the self-placed cause of your miserable plight? Who is to blame, if not yourselves? It is as impossible for you as to pull down the heavens, to be really happy without loving God, and no extent of feigning will enable you to love Him, if you keep not His commandments and the precepts of His Church. Your faith, your hope, may be all that they should be in theory, but without the love of God they are utterly dead; only when God's love is in his soul are a man's faith and hope capable of bearing fruit. How much this virtue of the love of God should be prized by you, when your faith will have been satisfied by seeing, and your hope by possessing, your charity, if you will but love God in this life, must continue throughout eternity. Why, then, should any man in his senses shut out the love of God from his soul?

Why should you not now in good earnest deplore your past folly, and say once for all with honest hearts, each for himself, "now, my God, I begin to love You as I should have done long ago;" henceforth Your commandments and the precepts of Your holy Church shall be the sacred rules of my life. I have done a great violence to my soul, and a great injury to Your infinite majesty in excluding Your love from my heart; henceforth my heart shall be unreservedly Thine, O my God! Should you pass over this appeal made in the interest of yourself and the cause of your God, with cold indifference, as you have so often done before; should you continue to think as little of loving God and being loved by Him as you have in the past, I must confess that I cannot imagine greater objects of pity than you. But you, dear people, whose consciences proclaim that you love God in the observance of His commandments, and the precepts of His Church, in fidelity to the duties of your respective states in life, in your horror for sin, in your exactitude in avoiding its occasions, in vigilance, in prayer, in pious reading, and zeal for His cause, remember that there are degrees of His love in the human heart, and you should earnestly aspire to attain the highest. Be generous in your love of God; stop not at the mere fulfilment of duty, but always show the happy disposition so well expressed in the lives of these saintly ones who are now looking down upon us from the galleries above, whose blessed motto in God's service was rather to do more than less. As it was for them, this happy disposition will be for you a most valuable contributor to the feast of a good conscience, and a most faithful mollifier of all difficulty you may experience in observing the criterion of God's love in the soul—the keeping of the commandments. "He who has My commandments and keeps them, he it is who loves Me."

XII.

FIRST SUNDAY OF LENT.

THOSE WHO DELAY THEIR CONVERSION.

"Behold, now is the acceptable time: behold, now is the day of salvation."—2 Cor. vi. 2.

In the whole course of our rational life, at no time are we free from the obligation of laboring for our salvation. The present season, however, is one in which we have special obligations to make use of extraordinary holy means to that end, which, when devotedly complied with, are followed by a rich return of heavenly favors that greatly promote our cause. Therefore, the Lenten season is called by the Church in the language of the Apostle "the acceptable time." Whilst there are those in every parish who will, to the full, take advantage of the richness of the season, there are those who will only partially do so, and unfortunately there are some who will pay no more heed to the obligations of this season than they do to their Christian duties at any other times—which is none at all. These form the class of nominal Catholics who are only too common, and whose unchristian lives are heartrending to the priest of every parish. They live as if they had no obligation, as if they had no souls to save, no hell to avoid, no heaven to gain. Are there some such in this congregation? If so, in God's name let them give ear to what I have to say, for every word will be for their special benefit. May the good God grant that they will carry away some impression that will awaken in them an earnest desire to choose this as "the acceptable time" for their reconciliation with their long insulted God!

What, O men! do you mean? If you continue to abuse the infinite mercy of the good God, you egregiously expose yourselves to the awful risk of dying in hardened impenitence, or of being cut off without time to say: "God have mercy on you." Surely you have not concluded to end thus. If you have, why are you here? What business have you in God's Church if you have concluded to give yourselves to the devil in time and eternity? Perhaps you are of the number that think they can treat God as they please, as if He were a stick or a stone; that think they can continue insulting Him to the very door of hell, contenting themselves with some incidental signs of religion, and then, as if God were a menial servant that should obey their every beck, He must, by the absolution of the priest, forgive them all, and from the very door of hell catch them up into heaven. My dear people, do not deceive yourselves. No Catholic questions that the absolution of the priest is all powerful to forgive the sins of the sinner, no matter how numerous or grievous they may be, providing that the person has the requisite dispositions. But how can we suppose that a man who heeds not God's warnings, but continues to insult Him as long as he is able, and then only pretends to change when he thinks death is upon him, has the requisite dispositions for forgiveness? It is true, God's mercy is infinite, and He extended the grace of repentance to the dying thief on the cross.

This, however, is the only certain recorded instance we have of true repentence and forgiveness in death after a continuous life of sin. Reasons, too, could be given to show that even in this instance the poor man on the gibbet had many circumstances in his favor, calling for divine clemency to which the Catholic man instructed in his religion and having every facility to practise it, has no claim whatever. Many indeed are the cases of sickness of sinners in which the priest and themselves conclude that the last has come, but contrary to the expectations of both, after the seeming repentance, health is eventually regained. What follows? In the majority of such instances the persons return to their former wicked ways. Were they sincere? Remember that the very soul of repentance is a resolution to lead a good life, should they have it in their power to do so. It requires no slight strain of the imagination to conclude that they were sincere. If they were not, what then would have been the result had they gone out of life? Simply this, that before their bodies would have been cold, their souls would have gone with God's curse to their places in hell. God saw this, and because of His infinite mercy, appealed to, perhaps, by the prayer of a pious mother, or a religious wife, or a devoted child, either in the flesh or in the spirit, before His throne in heaven, He gave them another opportunity. "God wills not the death of a sinner, but that he be converted and live." But such sinners seem to have no use for God or His priests, save to trifle with them when they think the last has come; trifle, I say, for their subsequent lives seem to show that their seeming repentance was nothing short of trifling with God and the priest, even in what they deemed death. Nay worse, in that most awful moment, it would seem, they lied to God and the priest who exacted of them a promise that, should their lives be spared, they would lead good Christian lives in future. I speak plainly, for this is not the place for studied rhetorical expression. Now all this, though awful as it may seem, is not a matter of surprise to one who will give serious thought to what conversion after a life of sin means. Have you who have been delaying your repentance ever given the matter a serious thought? It seems you have not. In God's name do so now.

Within you palpitates a heart corrupted with habits of sin; a heart that has constantly resisted God's inspirations; a heart that is an utter stranger to the love of God, and that has withstood in its stone-like hardness all the most powerful motives advanced to soften it into compunction. Is it likely that such a heart changes in a moment? Who in his senses will advance that, when the body is racked and the mind distracted in the agonies of death, is a propitious time for this change on which depends all for which life is worth living? Bear in mind that the life-work of uttering acts of contrition and love is not an unmistakable sign of a change of heart. The work of conversion would be quite an easy task if a sinner after insulting God, as long as he has strength to do so, could by a few cold acts acquire the dispositions for the sacraments, without which they will prove so many sacrileges. Be not deceived, you who are deeply concerned in this matter. The work of conversion to God means much more than that. As I have already said, it means an entire change of heart, and this means that God, Who has for many years been contemned and set at naught, must with the whole heart be loved above all things. That the idol of the heart swayed by passion, which has been cherished for so long, must be hated and detested. Are man's last moments the proper time in which to effect all this? Do you find that you can, at will, love or hate the same object, and transfer your affections and aversions in a few moment's notice? No; this is not the experience of any man in the full use of his reason. Besides, God's grace never forces a man's will; it aids when he co-operates, and co-operate he cannot even without grace. Does the man who persists in insulting God to his last breath, act like a man on whom the grace of co-operation is likely to be bestowed? Ah, no.

You must see, then, in these few remarks, unfortunate man, who has been delaying your repentance, what a stupid life you have been leading. In God's name then, put a stop to your stupidity. Make the one thing that should concern you safe by an honest and peace-giving confession. "This is the acceptable time," hear God's word telling you to make use of it. "Delay not to be converted, and put it not off from day to day." Too long have you done this.

XIII.

SECOND SUNDAY OF LENT.

THE CHRISTIAN'S DUTY AS EXPRESSED IN THE SIXTH COMMANDMENT.

" For this is the will of God, your sanctification: that you should abstain from fornication."—1. Thess. iv. 3.

In this sentence the Apostle reminds Christians of their positive and negative duty as expressed in the Sixth Commandment. The contrast is not greater between the brightest and most beautiful angel in heaven, and the most foul and loathsome spectre of hell, than that which exists between what this commandment exacts and what it forbids. Christians are bound by it, as by the other commandments, to labor for their sanctification. The more they advance in this, the more they become like the angels, and the nearer they approach the angels, the purer in thought and desire, in word and action, in body and soul, they become. " Purity bringeth its possessor near to God." No one, whatever may be the circumstances, but is held to the practice of this virtue. Virginal chastity is the virtue of those who have vowed to follow the Lamb in time and in eternity, but law-abiding purity is the virtue of all who aspire no higher than to keep the commandments. The nuptial bond is an emblem of the hallowed union which exists between Christ and His Church, and therefore it should never be tarnished by thought or desire, by word or action, contrary to God's law. The prayers of the unmarried should constantly ascend to the throne of the most High, asking for aid to perserve in scrupulous fidelity to its practice. In a word, human life, or the miser's hoard, should not be guarded with greater precaution and more vigilance than this virtue by every Christian. It is a beautiful chariot which carries the soul upward to the God of all purity.

The soul of the Christian is the temple of the Holy Ghost; the body of the Christian is the perpetual shrine of the soul and the Holy Ghost, and the temporary tabernacle of the virgin body of Jesus Christ. By any departure from the virtue of purity, this living temple of the Holy Ghost, and this living shrine and tabernacle, are so sacrilegiously defiled as to become the rendezvous of the most foul spirits of hell. Should the departure involve another, the deplorable consequences are twofold, and greatly aggravate the fall and remorse of both. " Those who sow in the unlawful pleasures of their carnal nature, will reap bitterness and remorse." That these soul-crushing fruits are so common in the world, and even among Christians, shows but too well how common this most deplorable calamity is. At all times it has been one of the greatest curses of the human family, but since so-called justice, irrespective of God's law, has begun to pander to it, the outlook for the family, society, and good morals is, to say the least, appalling. Once the foul spirit of unlawful carnal pleasure takes possession of a soul, to dispossess him is admitted to be one of the greatest difficulties which the person wishing to return to God encounters. How often is it the sad lot of persons who, crazed with remorse and bitterness, make some efforts to free themselves from their thraldom only to fall more deeply into his meshes. Their motive is not good; their efforts are but half-hearted, and therefore he holds sway. They would gladly take refuge from the bitterness and remorse, but they still love their unlawful pleasures. So long as this continues their case is hopeless, and gradually assumes more alarming phases till, alas! only too often it ends in impenitence, or dementation, or suicide. Great God, protect our people from such a calamity!

Hence it is not only the incumbent duty, but also the very great interest of all, whether young or old, married or single, to be ever well-armed against this monster, always on the alert to effect an entrance into souls. Without such arms as all Catholics have at their disposition, if they will but use them, he is sure to conquer. Unaided with divine succor, man would in vain hope to withstand the tax of the impure spirit, especially since his own flesh and the world conspire with the evil one to effect his ruin. Being then always well-armed, he must be both prompt and earnest in resisting his first onslaughts. When the resistance lacks promptitude or earnestness, an impression of a greater or less degree is made, and if the evil one follow that up, which he is sure to do, the victory will be his. Once he succeeds in effecting in the heart the merest taste for sinful carnal pleasures, he will soon have the whole man within his power, to carry him whithersoever he pleases. All lustful thoughts then should be banished from the mind with as great celerity as the burning spark is brushed from the hand. The thought is the forerunner of the desire, and when the former is at

all allowed to lurk, the latter is not far distant. The
senses, those windows of the soul through which both
bad and good impressions are conveyed, cannot be too
carefully guarded. Because of the downward tendency
of our nature, impressions of an evil nature are much
the easier made, and much the more difficult to exclude.
They are as sulphurous tinges upon the soul, which
gradually prepare her for the fire of lust. Who that
cautiously fortifies himself against the enemy of purity, has not experienced how important it is to guard
his eyes? Oh, how many souls that were once pure
and beautiful in the sight of Heaven, are now in hell
through unguarded glances at suggestive objects! The
admonitions of the holy scriptures, the recorded examples of the holy ones of the scriptures, the scrupulous care and emphatic advices of the saints, coupled
with our own experience, leave no room for quibble as
to the importance of guarding our sense of seeing.
David furnishes a sad example of how easy it is to fall
from a high degree of virtue into this most abominable
vice. Little, if any less careful should one be in
guarding his sense of hearing. The evil one seems to
give inspiration after his own fashion to his slaves to
dilate in the most attractive style on subjects fraught
with the greatest danger. The vile charm of the serpent seems to convey itself with every word they utter
for the ultimate ruin of the hearers. Fly from such
vile oracles as you would from the appearance of the
monster whom they represent. Employ not your
tongues in relating to others their soul-ruining conversations, falsely deeming it to be no harm to re-tell what
you have heard. Remember that the heart of the person cannot be pure who employs his tongue in even

relating impure conversations which he has heard. "From the fulness of the heart the mouth speaketh." And again: "Evil communications corrupt good morals." If by straws we can determine the wind's direction, by conversations we discover a man's inclinations. An idle, soft life is most ill-becoming a follower of our blessed Lord and His saints, and is most favorable for the attacks of the evil one. The body, the mind, should be usefully employed according to one's circumstance. Who does not find by experience that the time when his mind is not fruitfully engaged, is one in which evil thoughts cost him most trouble? Let no one presume on his own strength so far as to have recourse to associations and resort to places that prove occasions of temptations. God's aid will not be wanting to us when in His cause, or in the discharge of our duty we encounter temptations, but His succor we cannot expect in self-imposed dangerous occasions. His word to us is to fly such occasions, and if we fail to obey Him, it is clear we love them, and His word again is that: "He that loves the occasion shall perish in it."

Sufficient has been said for any one to see how greatly it concerns him to obey the voice of the Apostle, reminding us that it is the will of God that Christians should aspire to their sanctification by excluding whatever might tend to destroy the virtue of purity. "For this is the will of God, your sanctification," etc.

XIV.

THIRD SUNDAY OF LENT.

" Let no man deceive you with vain words."—Ephesians v. 9.

Experience will not allow any one to doubt of his proneness, when unguarded, to abuse his faculty of speech. Hence, the virtuous have always deemed it one of their most important duties to keep a strict control over this faculty. It is a power in good or in evil. The Apostle, knowing this, cautions us in the words of our text not to be deceived by the vain and delusive words of those who abuse this faculty in the cause of evil. Since but the comparative few in every community aspire with true Christian earnestness to the practice of virtue, it is not hard to imagine how wide-spread is the abuse of man's power of speech. Because it is so, we must feel that the Apostle had good reason to put the faithful on their guard. People who are not religiously inclined are not apt to have fair words for duties to them quite distasteful. They may not, for shame sake, assail them directly, but they fail not to attain their point in a circuitous way. One will assert that it is to him preposterous to expect people to fast; another will ridicule the idea of attending church so often; a third will, in his foolhardy fashion, fly in the face of God by saying that these practices are all very well for those who have no better way of employing their time, but for him there is little time for such nonsense. Are there not people here who have heard such expressions from the lips of so-called Catholics? Aye, and not unfrequently are such utterances made by godless men in the presence of children and the impressionable young. But hear these men dilate on matters of a worldly nature, nay, dare to listen to them on vicious topics, and you will perceive them all aglow with the charm of their subjects. Can one, who has a Christian sense of his duty, listen with any profit to the ravings of such people? Ah, no; but not unfrequently he leaves a far worse man than when he entered their vile company. It would, indeed, be a blessing if every community were so Catholic as to make such vicious characters feel that they are accounted its disgrace, by carefully shunning their vile company, till such time as they would change from their pagan like unseemliness to Christian propriety. But this is to speak of the impossible. Such godless blotches on the fair name of Catholicity in almost every community there are, and will be, till time will be no more. If we cannot shame them, we should, at least, protect ourselves by avoiding their society, and thus make them feel that self-respecting Catholics, at least, contemn their ways. Besides these disgraceful fossils, there are people whose tongues are so versatile that they can personate the saint and the sinner in almost the same breath. From their lips proceed expressions of sanctity that would do credit to the greatest saint, and expressions of evil that would shock us, coming from the vilest pagan. Could it be possible that they, according to the words of scripture, speak from the fulness of the heart in both roles? Ah, no; as the saint, they play the hypocrite, but in their wild unseemly expressions they are in their true role. Their tongues are at times lent to communicate to innocent souls in delicate circumstances the knowledge of God-cursed practices that but too often tell against life, both of body and soul. Oh, how many can rue the day that they lent ear to the serpent's charm that came from such vile tongues; how many tender souls will never see the face of God in glory, because of the scandal given their mothers by such wicked tongues! What a blessing it would have been for those mothers, and their children, had they in time exclaimed with the holy one of the scriptures: "O Lord, deliver my soul from wicked lips, and deceitful tongues." The expression, too, of the psalmist might have been most fruitfully pronounced by those, who instead of suing for God's aid to escape the scandalous effect of immoral tongues, lent, unfortunately for themselves, willing ears to the smooth speech and alluring words of those bent on their ruin. Had they, true to the cravings of their better nature, sought aid from above, they would, when the occasion presented itself, have stood for their virtue and the honor of their sex, and expressed in their conduct the true and only real beauty of woman, by indignantly spurning the one who would dare, in their presence, wound modesty.

There is, it is to be deplored, in almost every community, a class of young people who deem it smart not to be over particular in their violations of religious duties, and who, to the very great encouragement of others in evil, make light of serious matters. They are ever willing to lend their voice to counsel others in their doubts, not failing of course, to pander in woful deference to their likes and dislikes, no matter how telling against virtue. They are experts in the art of flattery, and not unfrequently the giddy-headed suffer a species of intoxication from their designing plaudets for every trifle which makes them pliable minions. In this way the more advanced in years lead their juniors who have not yet forfeited all the good effects of religious training. Serious evil is made light of, doubts are solved satisfactorily to the willing victim, and the young head is turned by extravagant flattery, and at length, God and religion are matters of the past in the young person's life. This is the process which effects the religious ruin of so many young people. No sooner have they passed their majority than they are caught up as companions to the more advanced, to be led on by flattery and encouragement to God only knows what end.

Oh, how many of both sexes have to rue the day that they made the acquaintance of such companions. Happy would it have been for them had they judged those new-found associates according to their betrayal of a disregard for virtue. What a world of misery the evil tongues of men are capable of producing! The unrestrained tongue sways a most powerful influence over the morality of its unhappy possessor. It seems to dash him into most ill-becoming and extravagant excesses. It brings to bear on him a species of intoxication which so robs him of his better sense that after the mischief has been done, he is amazed at himself. This is a common disease with those who are lacking in a true spirit of religion, and since, alas! they are by far the majority of every community, it only shows how much it behooves us to be on our guard. We should always be cautious not to encourage detracting and calumniating tongues, and never be so devoid of charity as to retell what, perchance, they may have uttered against their neighbors. The fact of the subject of the detractor being true does not give him a license to communicate it to others, and much less to one that has aught of regard for his obligation of charity. But the calumniator's tongue should be dreaded as much, if not more, than the burglar who is content with your money, which is much inferior in value to your character. Shun such tongues, always bearing in mind that as they treat others, so will they deal with you. Remember that, were there no listeners, there would be no calumniators, nor detractors. How, then, can one who encourages them in their nefarious traffic feel that he is excused from participation? Did they meet a timely reproof, they would be slow to try their wares on others, and many a serious trouble and enmity might be avoided. St. James pronounces "the man's religion vain who bridles not his tongue." So, too, will our religion become vain if we obey not the admonition of St. Paul, but allow their words to deceive us.

From this short consideration, it seems clear that we have great reason to be on our guard against the wicked tongues of men. Carelessness in this important matter will ere long make us the sorry victims of a most damning deception but too commonly the lot of some who would have otherwise proved devoted Christians. "Let no man deceive you with vain words."

XV.

FOURTH SUNDAY OF LENT.

"So then, brethren, we are not the children of the bond-woman, but of the free: by the freedom wherewith Christ has made us free."—Galatians iv. 31.

When our blessed Lord ascended the heights of Calvary and offered Himself on the cross for the sins of men, a freedom burst upon the world, which only God could give to man. The emancipation was to a man complete, and man could walk again upon the face of the earth in the full enjoyment of the liberty of a child of God. This freedom, purchased at such infinite cost, is one of God's most signal favors to man. Without it, man's self-inflicted slavery would have been his portion in time and in eternity, and all the other gifts of God would have proved parties to its bitterness. But who that has a thought of the slavery from which man has been ransomed can contemplate without sorrow the millions that still continue in that bondage, as if the price of their redemption had not been paid; the millions that reach but the first fruits of liberty and advance no farther, and the millions that were in a condition to enjoy all that the freedom of the children of God signifies, but of their own free choice, cast themselves into another species of slavery little less dangerous? As you must be aware, I refer to the unbaptized millions on the face of the earth, to the millions that received baptism, but nothing more, and to the millions of bad Catholics throughout the world. All who are not of these enjoy that blessed "freedom with which Christ has made us free."

Hence it is clear that by far the larger number are yet slaves of their own free choice, and but the few enjoy the liberty purchased for them by the most precious blood of Jesus. Since then, the inhabitants of the earth have freely divided themselves into two classes, we behold marching in one direction the children of liberty, and in another the children of bondage. The former enjoy heirship to the kingdom of God, their Father; the latter forfeit it, so long as they choose to groan under the bonds of their slavery. The children of freedom are not willing to forfeit their heirship to heaven, to walk in the way of the children of bondage, and the latter are not willing to break with the imagined pleasures of their way, to gain heirship to heaven. So, agreeably to the expression of Scripture, they travel towards eternity on two roads. The inhabitants of the earth are on either of these roads, as we are told by God's word. One is broad, and traversed by the many, and the other is narrow, on which but the few make journey. The broad road, as is well-known to all, terminates in regions of eternal misery so great as to surpass all that the human eye has seen, or the human ear has heard, or the human heart has conceived. But as all likewise know, the narrow road leads up into regions of bliss, the like of which, says St. Paul, "neither eye hath seen, ear heard, or heart of man conceived." So with the knowledge, from God's word or from interior visitations, of the circumstances of the end of their journey, they speed away in their different directions, with some exceptions of persons passing through sin or repentance, from one road to the other.

One of the chief reasons why such a great multitude walk in the broad road which terminates in the region of everlasting despair, is their utter lack of serious thought of aught beyond this world. "With desolation is the world made desolate, because people do not think in their hearts." They shut out, as if they consider them mere fiction, all thought of the most solemn truths taught the world by God. They set themselves against the light, and in fact, as Our Lord expresses it, they hate the light that would set them free." Thus blindly they journey on without thought, save for the present. The world and its toys are the idols to which they give their lives, irrespective of consequences. But of all, the most inconsistent that thus blindly ruin themselves, are the Catholics who made solemn profession to take the narrow road consecrated by the footprints of Our Lord, and hallowed by the tread of their forefathers. In the most solemn manner they vowed their willingness to follow Christ and to live by the maxims of His gospel, but contrary to their vow, they have deserted their Leader, refused to follow their forefathers, and rejected the maxims of the gospel for those of the world found on the broad road. They have bartered liberty for slavery, happiness for misery, heaven for hell, and God for the devil. Good God, what an exchange they have made!

How refreshing it is to turn from the contemplation of those that are, unfortunately for themselves, on hell's highway, to the consideration of the lives of faithful children of God's Church. In them we find the true principle of a Christian life, which is love for

God above all else. This love is stronger than death, therefore no sacrifice is considered too great when God's honor or glory is at stake. In God and for Him their charity in all its phases goes out unstintedly to their fellow-man, irrespective of his circumstances, of color, nation or creed. Their thought, their word, their action are all in perfect harmony with the demand of Our Lord: "If you wish to be my disciples, have love one for another." This is the true badge of the Christian school, and as they are its pupils, without it they are never found. They are never forgetful that, were it not for God's grace, they too would be numbered amongst those on the highway to destruction. Fresh in their memory is always the recollection of their own inability, and of their capability with God's grace. On all occasions and in all circumstances God's holy will is theirs, or should they, by sudden outbursts of complaining nature, be betrayed into faults against this rule, they are repented of as soon as committed. They are clear sighted to their own defects, and on account of them, with true Christian sincerity, they despise themselves. The stings of self-love are met with the wholesome salve of self-denial, and the fragments of the cross of our blessed Lord, which fall to their lot, are most cheerfully embraced. "Many are called, but few are chosen," and who will not grant that these are the unquestionable signs of the chosen? As we are all aware, there are, of course, degrees in the exercise of these holy duties to which all do not attain, yet all of the school of Christ practise them in a greater or less degree. Thus live those who enjoy "the freedom wherewith Christ has made them free."

It is for us, dear people, during this blessed season

of partial retirement, to judge for ourselves as to which road we may be traversing. The distinction is so great between the two classes that it should not be difficult for one to conclude. Should there be one in this congregation whose conscience upbraids him for being on hell's highway, let me beg of him to lose no time in effecting a change. But to all those who can happily claim to be the liberty-blessed children of God, let me say that the highest degree of Christian perfection should be their constant aim. The cause is abundantly worthy of their best efforts.

XVI.

PASSION SUNDAY.

"Neither by the blood of goats, or of calves, but by His Own blood, entered once into the Holies, having obtained eternal redemption."—Hebrews ix. 12.

When the angels sinned against their God, He exercised towards them to the full the rigors of His justice in banishing them into its dismal everlasting regions. We, in the person of the parents of our race, became their fellow-criminals, but His mercy vied with His justice and obtained for us the compromise, full of consolation, of a promise of a Redeemer. During the long night of four thousand years this promise was the hope and great consolation of the children of the old Dispensation. Throughout that long span of years, the Redeemer promised was familiar to the people under titles such as the "Messias," "He Who was to come," "the Desired of Nations," "the Desired of the eternal hills," "The Saviour," "the Just One," and others. The condition of the compromise agreed upon by God's justice and His mercy was, that adequate satisfaction should be made to His justice. The dishonor offered His divine majesty was infinite, therefore the satisfaction should be nothing less. To redeem us, then, required one whose ransom would be infinite, and as none but a God could pay such a wonderous forfeit, a God was to be our Redeemer—the God, Jesus Christ, Whose most precious blood had been so long prefigured by the blood of goats and the blood of calves. His blood was thus prefigured, not because the shedding of His blood was necessary to repair the injury caused to the infinite majesty of His Father by man's transgression, but for the reason that He would go through the terrible stages of His Sacred Passion, shed His blood, and die, having so decreed for His own blessed ends from eternity. One act of His will, one word, one action, because of its infinite value, and the infinite honor accruing therefrom to the majesty of His Father, would in the strictest justice have been abundantly sufficient to redeem the human race. Among the reasons which He had for embracing the terrible sufferings of His Sacred Passion and death, doubtless were to induce us to love Him, and to convince us of the pre-eminent value of salvation. The effects, therefore, which every review, no matter how cursory, of His great sufferings in His Sacred Passion and death should have on us, are increased love for Him, and a higher conception of the value of our eternal salvation.

A man cannot show greater love for his fellow-man than to give his life for him. In the present instance He Who gives His life is infinitely more than man, He is God, the Son, co-equal with His Father. When, then, we keep in mind His infinite dignity, and man's infinite inferiority; when we recollect the fact that man, far from being a friend, was His enemy; when we entertain the conception that He had at the time and from all eternity in His divine mind, that the vast majority of mankind would continue for time and eternity to be His enemies, and yet embraced His sufferings and death, it is impossible for us not to see an infinite love displayed, and an infinite price paid for our ransom in even the slightest circumstance of His passion and His death. Imagine then, if you can, the infinite riches which He contributes to the treasury of His Church, to be drawn therefrom by her faithful children till the end of time, by suspending, as it were, the infinite bliss of His divinity, to allow His humanity to be seized with the mortal anguish of the garden. Till we are face to face with Him on the great judgment day, we will have but a very imperfect knowledge of the great sufferings of Our Lord in this, or in any other stage of His Sacred Passion. It is infinitely beyond us to have full conceptions of the sufferings of Him Who is God, as well as man, in such circumstances. To us they may seem no greater, but in some respects even less than many of the martyrs underwent, whilst, because of the difference in the persons, they are in every respect infinitely greater. How vain it is, then, for us to endeavor to have a full conception of the extent of the fear and sorrow with which He allowed Himself to be seized whilst on His way to Gethsemane; how futile it would be for us to aim to have within the narrow compass of our most comprehensive thoughts, aught like a fair idea of the sorrow which the man-God experienced, when on entering the garden He shrank back, and exclaimed to His Apostles: "My soul is exceedingly sorrowful, even unto death!" Should we not, in view of such a scene, cry out: be astonished, O ye Angels! and tremble, O man! He before Whom the very pillars of heaven tremble; Who with a simple word gave existence to all things; Who rends the very heavens with thunder and lightning; and Whose omnipotent arm knows no limit, is seized with a mortal fear, is "sorrowful unto death!" Who could credit that the Author of life could be "sorrowful unto death," had He not spoken? What did He see in that solitary garden, where nature lay hushed in death-like silence, and clad in mourning, which His Apostles saw not? He saw each one of you, dear people; He saw me and every member of the human family, from Adam to the last on earth, arrayed on one side, about to lay their sins and abominations to Him to atone for them, and He saw the infinite justice of His eternal Father about to burst upon Him because of these sins and abominations, from another side. The awful volume of the future lay open to His divine mind in that garden. On its pages He beheld the crimes and blasphemies of ungrateful generations, and the legions of souls that would be lost, notwithstanding the infinite sacrifice He was about to make to afford all mankind the means to keep from sin and save their souls. So crushed was He at the awful sight, that the terrible sorrow which swayed Him burst the very pores of His virgin body, and forced therefrom a sweat of blood which purpled the very ground on which He lay. What but the infinite love of the Sacred heart of the God-man could surmount the provoking scenes of ingratitude on the part of those for whom He had begun to suffer, and was about to die, which loomed up in their most ghastly form before His divine mind in that solitary garden? He saw all mankind as His enemies, yet His love for all, even the very worst, constrained Him to most willingly commit His virgin body to the most cruel outrages, and to a most violent death for even the least and worst of mankind. For the least and worst, as well as the best, in compliance with the love of His Sacred heart, He with an ardent will, underwent in most minute detail, all the indignities, insults, and injuries which the malice of the inveterate enemies that surrounded Him in that garden could suggest. He allowed Himself to be ridiculed and condemned as a malefactor by the most iniquitous court that ever disgraced humanity. At the bidding of a cowardly pagan, who admitted His innocence in the same breath that he commanded the cruel outrage, our dear Lord gave His Sacred body to His enemies to be torn with scourges in the bloody flagillation at the pillar. He allowed them to treat Him in the most barbarous manner; to crown Him with thorns, mock Him as a pretender, expose Him all torn, bleeding, and disfigured to the heartless, surging multitude, load Him with a huge, rough cross, and finally put Him to a most violent death. All this He willed; He most ardently desired because of the infinitely intense love of His Sacred heart, not only for the good—for those who would in every age be found to acknowledge the infinite favor show gratitude for it, and duly apply its blessed fruits to their souls for their sanctification and salvation—but for even the very worst of the human family, for those would deny Him and ridicule Christianity. Oh the infinite love of the Sacred heart of Jesus Christ for poor, ungrateful man! For all this, what He asks in return is the poor heart of man—"Son, give Me thy heart."

XVII.

PALM SUNDAY.

HUMILITY AS TAUGHT BY OUR LORD.

"He humbled Himself, becoming obedient unto death, even the death of the cross."—Phillippians ii. 8.

Only the humble practically belong to the school of our blessed Lord here below, and only the humble will enjoy His blessed presence in the regions of bliss above. We are practical followers of Our Lord so long as we preserve the life of grace in our souls; this we cease to do when all humility departs, for: "God rejects the proud and gives His grace to the humble." When proud and rejected by God, of what are we capable? Certainly of nothing worthy of a follower of the humble Jesus. And if we are capable of nothing, what becomes of our hope? How can we repent? But, if we would enter heaven, we must both hope and repent—these we cannot do without some degree, at least, of humility. Is there one here who does not believe, as certainly as he does his own existence, that Baptism and Penance for the remission of mortal sin committed after Baptism are necessary for salvation? No, there is not; for a Catholic he could not be if he believed not in the necessity of these sacraments. But on whose authority do you believe in the necessity of these sacraments? On the authority of Him Who said: "Amen, I say to you, unless you be converted and humble yourselves as little children, you shall not enter into the kingdom of heaven." A proud soul cannot be the habitation of the Holy Ghost; a proud soul cannot enter heaven or abide in its ante-chamber from which the proud angels were hurled into the regions of God's avenging justice. God is the God of the humble; self is the god of the proud; God is loved above all things by the humble; self is loved above all else by the proud. To whom, then, should the reward be given; on whom should punishment be imposed? The foundation, the root, the spring of all that is Christian in man is humility.

The first lesson given by the Divine Author of Christianity was one in humility; the first words which came from His sacred lips, as He pronounced His famous sermon on the mountain, inculcated humility. The wickedness of the human race whom Our Lord came to redeem, had for its foundation, root and spring, pride, deep-seated pride, which was inherited from the first Adam, as the fruit inherits the disease of the tree. Becoming, therefore, was it that the followers of the second Adam should inherit from Him humility, the foundation, root and spring of all Christian virtue. The first lesson, then, which we must learn from Our Lord is one in humility. Till we have, in some degree at least, acquired humility, in vain will we pretend to learn any other. Its necessity, as that which must rest beneath all the virtues of a Christian soul, is so indispensible that all His followers must learn it of Him: " Learn of Me, for I am meek and humble of heart." His whole blessed life was one continual lesson of humility. The gospels abound in records of His exercise of it, which, when we give thought to His infinite dignity, appear grand in the extreme. He found the world so intoxicated with pride as to worship certain objects which were reputed rich and elevated. He, the Possessor of all riches and grandeur, made choice for His portion of what seemed despicable to a proud world. After a condescension which we can never understand till in the great hereafter displayed in assuming human nature, not to speak of His mother who, though rich beyond the children of men with the riches of heaven, was the poorest of the poor in the riches of earth, all that He selected as His was mean and low in the eyes of the world. His foster-father, St. Joseph, was a poor artisan who had to earn his bread in working at his trade. He chose as His birth-place the habitation of the brute, and that, too, the property of another. It pleased Him to confound a proud world by being born in the most destitute circumstances. Whilst proud man's infant son was delicately laid in a down-cushioned cradle, the divine Babe, God's Son, of His own choice was laid upon rough straw in a lowly manger. The proud world caressed the son of the proud man and lavished encomiums on his parents as he grew in body and waxed strong, but the Son of God lived the greater part of His blessed life unknown to the world, and in the most humble circumstances. The proud conduct themselves towards the poor and illiterate, as if they belong to an inferior race, aye, often as if they were no better than the irrational brood of creation. How often have the proud, when they could, treated them as they would not think of treating their pet animals? Was this not the appalling state of affairs when Our Lord came into the world and found man a slave to his fellow-man? Have we not, even in our own age of boasted civilization and Christianity, witnessed the monstrous abuse? But He Who came to set all mankind free from a far worse slavery than that of man to man; Who came to release us from the slavery of the devil, would teach us to deny no man that liberty with which his Creator had blessed him; would teach us, if we would follow Him, to esteem and befriend the poor and the lowly. In His public life, twelve poor, illiterate fishermen He made His bosom, His intimate friends and companions. Oh, how the proud of those days were scandalized at His selection! Is there less pride in the world of to-day? Is not the proud world of the nineteenth century scandalized at the humility of the gospel, which is the humility of Jesus? The poor and the lowly are despised and neglected; the humility of Christ is a mark of disgrace, and but too often laughed at and ridiculed by boasting blasphemers, who are hailed in all directions by thoughtless people delighting in the pride of irreligion. Riches were one of the great gods of the proud in the age in which Our Lord came upon earth; they are no less so in the age in which we live. But He, the Divine Author of Christianity, of Christian humility, had not of His own whereon to lay His blessed head: "The foxes have coverts and the birds of the air have nests, but the Son of man hath not whereon to lay His head." How marked the contrast between the humble, retiring modesty of the God-man, Wisdom itself, and the intoxicating pride of poor mortals who must have the world ring with the little they know; between Him Who with a word made all things spring into existence, washing the feet of poor fishermen, and the mortals who swelled with pride at their importance, lord it to exasperation over their dependants; between the sentiments of the Sacred heart of of Him Who said: "I seek not My own glory, I honor My Father.... If I glorify Myself, My glory is nothing," and the sentiments of the hearts of the proud whose own glory is the beginning and end of all they do! He at times charged the witnesses of His miracles to give them no publicity; but poor, proud mortals must have every seeming good they do wafted, if possible, to the four quarters of the globe. Honors He fled from as if so many evils; honors the proud fly to as if so many blessings. When "they would make Him King, He fled to the mountain;" when they would make the proud man king, he would fly into their midst. Proud mortals flaunt to the full in the midst of honors; the God-man, the Master by excellence of Christian humility, in the midst of honors wept tears of grief; the proud retaliate to "the death" when they can, for injury or insult, but the God-man, "when He was reviled, did not revile; when He suffered, He threatened not." Nay, without a murmur, He bore all the insults and injuries that devils could suggest and wicked men execute. But the sublime climax to His life of the most profound humility was reached when "He humbled Himself, becoming obedient unto death, even the ignominious death of the cross."

From these few thoughts on humility, as taught by our blessed Lord, we can easily infer how necessary this virtue is to His followers. He is "the way," and the virtue absolutely necessary to qualify us in our weakness to tread His hallowed footprints, is Christian humility in some degree at least. Oh, let us henceforth learn of Him humility: "Learn of Me, for I am meek and humble of heart."

XVIII.

EASTER SUNDAY.

A TRUE CONVERT.

"Therefore let us feast, not with the old leaven, nor with the leaven of malice and wickedness, but with the unleavened bread of sincerity and truth."—1. Cor. v. 8.

Whatever may have been the past life of any Christian, if he would henceforth conform to the teaching of the Apostle, his duty is apparent in the words of our text. If, like the prodigal of the gospel, he had cast off the sweet and salutary restraints of God his Father, and taken for his unfortunate portion a place among the slaves of the devil, the world, and the flesh, he has been feasting on the unsavory leaven of malice and wickedness. Should he now, at last, realize his egregious mistake, and sigh for the pleasure of a good conscience, and the return of happy relations with his long-deserted Father, his dispositions must be sincere and true. With them his return will be hailed with joy by God's court, and he will be admitted to feast his poor, hungry soul on the most blessed Eucharist, the infinite expression of God's love to man.

The first happy move of the sinner to conversion is when he stops to study the picture of himself, which God in His mercy lays before him through the medium of his conscience. With his study, disgust for himself and his manner of living grows apace. His desperate plunge from grace to sin, which is the nearest approach of which he is capable in this life, to that of the rebel angels from heaven to hell; the meanness, indignity and ingratitude of his violation of the plighted allegiance on his reception into the Christian ranks; the number, the malice, the iniquity, the enormity of his sins; the graces abused; the thread between him and everlasting pain and misery; the forfeit of peace here and eternal happiness hereafter; and an infinitely loving Father desiring his return and willing to forgive him, are all made clear to him in the light of God's mercy, which illumines his conscience. This first move is then, clearly an effect of God's grace, and all his subsequent steps heavenward, till his confirmation in grace in the great hereafter, will be effects of the same cause. Next comes the act of his will to return to grace, but this, without the power of execution, would remain sterile. The gratuitous aid which enabled him to take the preceding steps will not be wanting to him to complete the work. With the view of himself, which God's grace afforded him through the mirror of his conscience, he has learned sufficient from his moral deformities to fill him with real sorrow for the enormity of his conduct towards God. The idols which his heart worshipped in his sinful wanderings become truely hateful, and but God receives its whole love. The change is even now complete, though yet it has to be sacramentally ratified and sanctified. Though the experience of his past weakness causes him to tremble, and his temptations have been numerous and powerful, he derives courage in his project for the future from his implicit confidence in God. He is convinced that God will not allow him to be tempted above his strength, and that for the mere asking, God's aid he will have. "God will not suffer you to be tempted above that which you are able." "For everyone that asketh, receiveth." Why, then, it may be asked, do so many seeming penitents become the sport of their enemies by relapses in which their last case proves worse than the first? My answer is this: either they lacked confidence in God at first, and therefore could not have had a firm purpose to sin no more mortally, or, in time of need, they neglected to ask for His aid, or they showed a want of will to use it by exposing themselves to the dangerous occasions of sin. The true penitent's purpose is founded on his confidence in God, which supposes a determination to constantly sue for His aid, by prayer and fidelity to Christian duties, and to avoid, as far as possible, all dangerous occasions of sin. After the penitent has been wrought up to these dispositions, the sacramental work really takes place in a good Confession. The genuine penitential spirit with which he is actuated, insists on this being as thorough as if, immediately after it, he should have to appear before the eternal Judge to have his lot forever decided. He condemns himself before his confessor in as plain and as full a detail of all the deformities of his conscience as he can command. He would gladly lay open the book of his conscience to him, as clearly as it is seen by God, if he could. The thoroughness with which he discharges this most solemn duty would seem to show that he takes a holy delight in condemning himself, and that he is determined that, not only will his guilt be forgiven and the eternal punishment remitted, but that also all temporal punishment will be blotted out by that confession. Oh, would to God that all who after years of sinful wanderings make a move to return to grace, possessed such worthy dispositions! Then, indeed, so many would not return, like the recently-washed swine, to the mire, to plunge themselves again into the filth of sin, or the sacraments would not be so often abused. Alas! but too often is it the painful lot of the priest to witness such sad relapses, or to discover subsequent signs, which fill him with horror, lest the sacraments had been abused!

Once the true penitent turns to God, he remains with Him. The grace which effected his conversion he never forfeits or forgets; he makes it the occasion of lifelong thanks to God. Henceforth his life is in line with his solemn vow made at the foot of God's altar; he is in truth a disciple of Christ. This is the one great aim of his life, to which all else must conform. Well does he know from sad experience, that as well might he pretend to fly as to presume to carry out his aim without fidelity to his religious duties in private, as well as in public. Conscious of his past weakness, and of the time lost while he was a prey to it, he has concluded to make most strenuous efforts to acquire strength, and to make the very best use of the time left him. He has his uniform devotions with which he sanctifies each day; to the sacraments of Penance and Eucharist he has frequent recourse; prayer is constantly in his heart and upon his lips; and good reading gets much of his spare time. If his circumstances in life be those of the poor and the humble, he thanks God that his portion is that sanctified by the blessed life of Jesus. Are there those who depend on him for support? in a true spirit of penance, he is faithful to his trust in providing for them. If he be blessed with means, he realizes that all he has belongs to God. Now that he has begun a new life, he views the goods of this world with other eyes. They are in his possession in trust; he is but the steward, who will have to give to God, their owner, a most strict account of the use he will have made of them. His study then, is to dispose of them according to the good pleasure of God. As in the past they were to him the occasions of sin, henceforth they must be a means of doing good. As in the days of his sinful wanderings they served him to plunge the deeper into expensive vices, now they must aid him to advance to higher degrees of virtue. Like his other talents, which he so long prostituted to vice, they must henceforth be used as becomes a follower of Christ.

In these few thoughts, dear people, we have a short outline of a true conversion from sin to grace. This is the change which St. Paul, and our Mother, the Church, would have all sinners undergo in this blessed Easter time. They should study themselves and their lives in God's holy light; they should resolve to return to a life of grace, and co-operate with the aid which God holds out to them, to execute their design. And when they will have risen with Christ, in a thorough confession, they should make use of the means, so as, like Christ, never to die again, save the death of the body, which is the lot of saint and sinner, and which, if they persevere, will be for them the happiest act of their lives on earth.

XIX.

FIRST SUNDAY AFTER EASTER.

" And it is the Spirit which testifieth that Christ is the truth."— 1. John v. 6.

Had God the Father not communicated to man, in words, that Jesus was His divine Son; had the testimony of devils and the possessed been omitted; had the dove not descended upon Him in the waters of the Jordan; had it pleased Him not to display His divine power in miracles, or permit them to accompany and follow His blessed death; had He even not appeared to man after His Resurrection, but invisibly ascended to heaven, the coming of the Holy Ghost as He had promised in His discourse after the Last Supper and His miraculous effects on all who received Him, would have sufficed to prove that Christ was God, and therefore Truth Itself. Not to dwell on the Holy Ghost's wondrous effects on the immediate disciples of Our Lord, or the grandeur which could only be of God, of His work in the Church instituted by Christ, if we be but good practical Christians, we have only to consult the Holy Spirit within us to know that Christ was God—Truth Itself.

Whilst clear it certainly is that some people are by nature virtuous compared with others, no less clear is it that it is the sad fashion of human nature to tend in a direction quite the opposite to that in which it would find itself if aided by divine grace—" The imagination and thoughts of man's heart are prone to evil from their youth." Human passions will gratify themselves to the full when not under control. Reason and self respect have but a partial and very unreliable power of restraint. They never can command for man complete, continuous control of his passions. In vain, therefore, will we expect to find a man master of himself among those who waive aid from on high, and rely for their success on reason and self respect. They may, it is true, seem to gain in some points, but on close investigation their progress often proves to be no greater than that of one vice taking the place of another, or the same vice under a different form, as in the case of Diogenes, when he trampled on Plato's curtains, and thus after his own fashion displayed the vice of which he would correct Plato. To subdue the passions, and bring them under complete control, a power infinitely greater than that which man finds in himself is absolutely necessary. For the man who has ever entertained a thought above nature, this ought not to be difficult to understand. What Christian man, who has ever given serious thought to his own weakness; who has ever prudently considered the numerous occasions that prove incentives to vice, the frequency and potency of temptations, and the world of vice-given natures around him, can be ignorant of this? Since such is most undoubtedly the case, would it not be presumption in the extreme for man, relying only on his own strength, to pretend to keep the commandments of God? Would it not too be on the part of God a clear case of expecting the impossible of His creatures were He not to put within the reach of man the means of acquiring the necessary strength? The rules which

Our Lord laid down for His followers are the means and the only means of acquiring this strength by which man can become master of himself and keep the commandments of God. This has been verified by every saint in heaven; to this every God-fearing person on earth will bear witness; and as negative testimony we have the unedifying, to say the least, lives of those who do not observe these rules. Therefore we have but to consult our interior to know that Christ, who gave these rules, and made them the mediums of a power that could only be of God, was God, and therefore Truth. Hence the words of Our Lord: " Whoever shall do my will shall know whether I am from God." The good Christian never could be what he is, if grace came not to him from the practice of those Christian duties which Our Lord marked out for all mankind. He must therefore say with St. Paul: " By the grace of God I am what I am." Every one here, who is so happy as to be a faithful child of the Church, has ample experience of this truth. Then let infidels and libertines prate as they may, the good Catholic has, besides the Church, which is God's infallible mouth-piece, his own heart telling him that only the great God could give him those means which afford him the strength to withstand the attacks of the devil, the sinful world, and his own corrupt nature. The staying power which keeps him as he is, onward and upward in the way of Christian virtue, could be no other than aid from God commonly called grace, which comes to him from the practice of his Christian duties.

Let a man be ever so good, should he become remiss in the observance of his Christian duties, he will soon experience a diminution of strength, and the gradual assertion of the overruling force of his passions. If his deterioration continue, ere long he will lapse into the dangerous state of lukewarmness, and finally end in entire neglect. When this sad condition is reached he ceases to be master of himself, or to prove equal to the grave responsibility of keeping God's commandments. And should his neighbor who had been held in disregard on account of his vices, be converted to God by the proper use of the means given by Our Lord to effect peace between God and the sinner, and continue true to the grace of his conversion in the practice of his Christian duties, he experiences a strength which enables him to control those passions which before had him for their slave, and a facility in discharging the grave obligation of keeping the commandments, which renders the solemn duty, utterly impossible in the past, easy. Hence the words of Our Lord: "The yoke is sweet, and the burden light." Whence could such strength come, save from God? When the teachings of Our Lord are obeyed, virtue is apparent; when they are disobeyed, vice is rampant. From the individual to the community, and from the community to all mankind, this is true. Let men flaunt as they please their so-called moves of reform, there is but one way to real reform, and that is for man to obey the teachings of Christ, whence will come a God-given strength to effect a true reformation in individuals and communities. Till this move towards God is made, neither the individual nor the community can hope for a real reform. But as sure as this is made by an individual or a community, so sure will purity, temperance, honesty and good principles spring up where the opposite vices had to be deplored. We move towards God in proportion to our fidelity to the teachings, of Christ, and by consequence we depart from Him in proportion to our infidelity to those teachings. No matter what vain men may say, it is clear that the hope, both of the individual and society, rests on fidelity to these teachings. By the power of God only, which is reached by this fidelity, can the individual and society hope to triumph over the vices that are, alas! but too common. Thus we see that the godless, as well as the God-fearing side of the human family, in a contrary way shows that Christ was God—Truth, who could communicate to a few simple duties the power to change a man from a devil to a saint; to make of a world of vice a world of virtue. All that remains to effect the reform is for man to avail himself of the power, by moving nearer to God in his fidelity to the teaching of Our Lord—God—Truth.

Hence it must be clear to those here, who may have been living in vice, that it has been their remissness in their Christian duties that has brought this calamity upon them. Our Mother, the Church, has been throughout the year urging them to return to a sense of their duty, but at no time are her appeals to them so strong as during this holy season in which it is their incumbent duty, as her children, to make their peace with God by a good sacramental Confession. Harden not your hearts against her voice, or you will be as the heathen and the publican—"He that will not hear the Church, let him be to thee as the heathen and the publican."

XX.

SECOND SUNDAY AFTER EASTER.

" Christ suffered for us, leaving an example that you should follow His steps."—1 Pet. ii. 21.

Our Lord of His own choice, in compliance with the will of His Father, suffered, thus leaving an example which all His followers, as far as their weakness will permit, should imitate. If therefore we would as we should walk in His hallowed footsteps, we must at least aim earnestly to bear the trials of life with resignation to the Divine will. In proportion as we show advancement in this conformity to God's will on all the trying occasions of our lives, will we resemble in our weakness, the perfect and all beautiful example of Christ, our divine Model. For love of us He suffered and died. What more sublime evidence of His love for us could He give than His sufferings and death? He, the eternal Son of God, clothed Himself with human nature, to suffer and die for us poor slaves! And shall we think it too much to bear with patience, for love of Him, the little crosses unworthy of the name that come upon us in the journey of life? If we love Him, as we most undoubtedly should, " we must take up our cross and follow Him." All pretensions to love Him, if we, unchristian like, refuse to carry our cross after Him, will be utterly without avail. What hardships people undergo, what trials they willingly encounter, and how they labor late and early, and spend themselves for aught that they value or love in this world. And shall we who have made solemn profession of following our blessed Lord, show that, after all He has done for us, we love Him not to the extent of bearing with Christian resignation a few little crosses each day for His sake?

We should remember that by outbursts of ill-governed temper in the trials of life, we not only act an ungrateful part towards Our Lord, but we besides frustrate God's eternal designs in our behalf. He has created and redeemed us for heaven, and He is constantly holding out to us the most effectual means to attain that end. Our daily trials may most certainly be classed amongst them, since without them we can never inhabit that "heaven which must be taken by storm." Would it not be a contradiction of the teaching of Our Lord were a responsible Christian able to gain possession of heaven without bearing his cross? Heaven was opened only by the cross of the Man-God, and every child of Adam was redeemed only by the cross of the Man-God; but to be saved, man must "take up his own cross and follow the Man-God." If there were another sure way to heaven, Our Lord would have certainly taught it to us. He taught us but one way in His blessed doctrine and example, and that is the way of the cross. "No cross, no crown" has always been a familiar phrase with the true followers of Our Lord. Till we, like them, allow this concisely-expressed truth to sink deep into our hearts, and have it bear the necessary fruit in our daily lives under the various little pressures we will be put to by our loving Father above, we cannot consider ourselves true followers of Our Lord. "Deny thyself; take up thy cross and follow Jesus," is the incumbent duty of all His true followers. Hence it is that the number of true followers of Our Lord is so small in every parish. Few are entirely satisfied. One has this to complain of; another has that which calls forth his murmurs, so that only the few are satisfied; the majority journey on towards eternity, displeased with God's disposition of matters in their regard. They rob themselves of the peace of contentment in this life, and expose themselves to the very great danger of being shut out from eternal peace.

What do they gain by this murmuring against God's will? Do they save themselves from a single cross? There could be no question of gain in such an unholy disposition. On the contrary their loss is thereby increased. The crosses they must experience, whether they will or not, and their ill-disposition makes them doubly heavy. Besides, they not only lose the merit which God intended they should gain by bearing their little trials in patience, but they actually commit sin by flying in the face of God. They are willing to bear all manner of trials, providing that in doing so they forward their worldly interests; but to suffer aught for Heaven is more than they can stand. This is the sad disposition of, alas! too many, even to the very moment of their death; nay, the older they become, the more they are willing to undergo for the things of earth, and the less disposed they seem to be to suffer anything in a spirit of Christian resignation to God's holy will. Yet these people are supposed to be animated with the spirit of Christianity which Christ gave to man; they are supposed to imitate His example as far as their weakness will permit; they doubtless, too, expect that God's promises will be made good in their behalf, as they have been in favor of all those who in every age bore their crosses in patience after our blessed Lord. "Patience is necessary for you, that doing the will of God you may receive the promise." They conduct themselves as if impatience were necessary to receive the promise.

Let us not deceive ourselves, dear people; we must, if we desire to enter heaven, carry our cross after Our Lord to its very door, for none save those who will have tried at least to bear with Christian resignation the "many tribulations" which cross them in this "vale of tears," will be admitted. They of whom we have spoken have not yet, to their own great loss, begun to try as they should. Let us not be so foolish as to imitate their very dangerous example, but let us henceforth work with all earnestness to walk, as near as our weakness will permit, in the blessed footsteps of Our Lord, by Christian submission in all our trials. The thoughts we have so far entertained should suffice to show us the inestimable value of resignation in the trials of life, and it is to be hoped that we now duly appreciate this virtue. Why should we not, therefore, set to work to acquire a virtue so necessary for our peace here and hereafter? We have nothing, indeed, to lose by acquiring it, but, on the contrary, everything to gain. Should we, like so many others, put ourselves to no trouble to acquire it, but continue to vent our anger or impatience at even the merest trifles, we will be our own worst enemies, as must seem clear from what has been said. Many, it is true, try to acquire this virtue, but their success seems slow. They deserve credit for trying, and thereby show that they have some disposition to be in line with all the true disciples of Our Lord. The slowness of their success rests with themselves. They have not yet begun to fully realize the great value of resignation to God's will. Hence they have yet to begin to desire it as something which, cost what it may, they must have; they have yet to begin to seek it as something of paramount importance; they have yet to begin to send up prayers for it that will attract, by their fervor, the attention of Heaven. This is why many so frequently show lack of this virtue under the pressures that come upon them. They desire it, they seek it, and they pray for it, but all in such a half-hearted way that their progress is scarcely perceptible. We must keep its great virtue, and the necessity we have of it, constantly before us, and then, like reasonable, candid Christians, we will set our hearts upon it and our wills to work to acquire it. Oh, how trifling our crosses are, how severe soever they may be in comparison with what we justly deserve for our sins! If, for one insult offered to God, all the penance that we could perform throughout eternity would be infinitely short of repairing the injury done, why shall we not deem ourselves fortunate when only the few crosses that befall us are exacted? How light they are compared with all Our Lord suffered! They are sent by our heavenly Father, whose desire to benefit us, both here and hereafter, is infinite. He knows what is best for us, and all His dispositions in our regard are most decidedly for our betterment. Not only the past and the present appeal to us to bow our heads in holy resignation to God, but also the future demands us to utilize those occasions of grace. Can we afford to throw away, by impatience, graces that we are sure to need to withstand the attacks of our spiritual enemies, for which the future, like the past, will not want? Let us therefore in future cheerfully submit to the divine will, and when we find our weakness inclined to assert itself, let us have recourse to earnest prayer. "Take up thy cross and follow Me."

XXI.

THIRD SUNDAY AFTER EASTER.

" That whereas they speak against you as evil doers, they may, by the good works which they shall behold in you, glorify God in the day of visitation."--1 Peter ii. 12.

It is an undoubted fact that the lives of, alas! too many Catholics in every community furnish the enemies of religion, and the unfriendly towards the Church, many sad occasions to ridicule the one, and give expression to their cants against the other. When prejudice already exists, every occasion is caught up and used to the most villainous advantage. By such biassed minds the ill-conduct of those wayward members of the Church is charged to religion and to the Church with a peculiar flourish of triumph. Hence, as in the days of the Apostles, it is found necessary to-day to cry out to Catholics not to disgrace their religion and their Church by ill-becoming conduct, but by their manner of living to edify their brethren, both within and without the Church. It is deplorable that so many hearken not to the warning voice, but continue in the evil tenor of their ways, as if none were concerned but themselves. They do not seem to realize that every self-respecting Catholic in the community is concerned, not indeed that he will have to account to God for the mischief wrought by the evil-doers, but because the occasions are furnished to the unfriendly to fling their canting insult at his Church. Many of those who thus bring ridicule upon religion and the Church, are the direct descendants of forefathers who bled and died to do them honor. Could they weep in God's kingdom above, they would certainly do so for being the forefathers of such unworthy descendants. Ah, that all Catholics would respect their religion and their Church; that they would refrain from disgracing their ancestors and their name; that they would have regard for the feelings of their Catholic neighbors; then indeed we would not have the very unseemly conduct of some to deplore. Oh, how many are disgusted, unfairly it is true, with religion, and kept out of the Church by the ill-conduct of bad Catholics! In this age of growing religious indifference only too many are not fair-minded enough to advert to the fact that such people are what they appear, not because of the religion they professed, which has peopled heaven with Saints, and will continue to do so till time will be no more, but emphatically because they do not practice what they once professed. In God's name, then, I beg of you whose conduct in the past has been scandalous or disedifying, to earnestly resolve on the contrary line of life in the future. See what mischief you have been doing to the cause, by excellence, of all of us. Resolve that your conduct will no longer be a blotch on this Catholic community, but that you will show those whom you have scandalized, by the becomingness of your future conduct, what you could have been in the past had you been faithful to the practise of your religion. You are now within the holy season in which it devolves upon you legally to make your peace with God. The voice of the Church has, since Lent began, gone out to you, and still contines to go out to you advancing the most powerful reasons why you should comply with this duty. Adding the present reasons to those which you must have heard in the past, you cannot but see that, from every point of view your life has been unworthy of one bearing the Catholic name. Resolve right now that your life shall be a worthy one in future, and ask your crucified God to bless your resolution, and furnish you with the grace to carry it into execution.

Whilst it is certain that the lives of bad Catholics do great mischief to religion and the Church in communities, no less certain is it that the edifying lives of good Catholics have no small part in disabusing non-Catholics of communities in which they live, of their unwarranted prejudices, and even not unfrequently attract them to the Church. Whilst the primary motives of every good Catholic, urging him to strict fidelity to all that his name implies, have direct respect to God and the salvation of his own soul, reflections from time to time on secondary motives, such as we are now engaged in, prove no small help to stimulate him to be most careful in his deportment, especially among those who are not children of the Church. He should not be slow to understand that amongst themselves they will comment on his ways as those of a Catholic. When, as we suppose, in the case of a conscientious Catholic, he disappreciates aught unbecoming in conversations; when his opinions are always found to be according to right reason and conscience, and when his entire conduct is not marred with any impropriety, but rather crowned with the public and faithful practise of his religion, it is needless to advert to what favorable impressions he will make. They cannot help, when admiring his ways, passing favorably on the Church to which he belongs. The favorable comments elicited by his upright life will go a great ways in proving to the most prejudiced that the ill-becoming life of his indifferent Catholic neighbor ought not, after all, to be charged to the Church, just as the becoming lives of children of any family home will prove to the most captious that the evil conduct of the "black sheep" of the family is not a consequence of his parental training. The lustre which their lives reflect upon their parents and home, to an extent, destroys the effects of his evil ways, and places the blame where it belongs—on himself.

No intelligent Catholic doubts that he has an obligation of charity, not only to refrain from whatever might tend to scandalize his neighbor, but to positively set him a good example. Charity binds us not only to refrain from doing our neighbor bodily harm, but also to aid him when he is in need, and to tender assistance when it is within our reach. Surely, then, charity obliges us to, at least, as much in respect to our neighbor's soul. There is no time in which edification will not prove beneficial even to the most God-fearing. Since such is most undoubtedly the case, it is easy to imagine what an amount of good an edifying life is capable of producing among those whose lives are not all they should be, among the indifferent and cold, and even among non-Catholics, and people who scarcely have any sense of religion. Persons necessitated to be in constant communication with such people should not forget this. I refer especially to those whose business relations lead them much amongst them; to those who may work in their midst, and to those who may find themselves constantly surrounded by them because of marriage relations. From these few remarks sufficient can be understood to enable us to realize the mischief done by the unchristian conduct of bad Catholics in every community afflicted with them, and the great good effected by the edifying example of good Catholics. Oh, dear people, never forget that you are children of God's Church, and let it never be said of you that you brought disgrace upon your mother by unchristian conduct. Let your example be worthy of your high vocation.

XXII.
FOURTH SUNDAY AFTER EASTER.

"For the anger of man worketh not the justice of God."—James i. 20.

Should we suffer at the hands of our neighbor, as Christians we should not allow ourselves to be blinded by the passion of anger and betrayed into the extremes of retaliation which it prompts. So far from being in keeping with God's justice, such passionate hearts disclose a disposition to assume the right of God to punish. Whilst it is the privilege of every man to defend himself and his rights, he should, however, do so, not after the fashion of those who become the slaves of anger, but in a Christian manner. Should his motives be purely to revenge the wrong which he really suffers or imagines he sustains, then a Christian spirit guides him not; he simply acts under the influence of a sinful anger. "Revenge is mine; I will repay," saith the Lord; the man who would thus act, asserts by his action that revenge is his, and that it is his right to repay. This surely is not to act a Christian part; it is quite another line of conduct from that which the blessed doctrine and example of Our Lord teach. Did He not teach us to forgive injuries; has He not made our forgiveness of injuries from others the basis of the forgiveness of those which we have committed against God?—"forgive us our trespasses, as we forgive those who trespass against us." "When reviled, He did not revile," but, on the contrary, when suspended between heaven and earth, a victim to the most excruciating torments, He prayed for those who crucified Him. It is true that it is not at all pleasant to nature to suffer the harsh treatment that some unreasonable, unscrupulous people, without reason, are guilty of towards their neighbors. But who is the more Christlike, the man who allows himself to be crazed with anger and rushes headlong, thirsting for revenge, or the man who, though keenly feeling the wrong done him, controls himself, nourishes no hard feelings, and conducts himself as if nothing contrary to his liking had occurred? We certainly could expect as much from the non-Christian, as the former betrays, but the way of the latter is truly Christian. It is needless to say that the Christian slave of anger is a stranger to the practise of meekness and humility, of mercy and peace, of patience and mortification, and yet he is bound to practice these virtues to a becoming degree. They are some of the beautiful virtues which Christ taught His disciples, and all who really are practical Christians are His disciples.

Anger is one of the capital sins. Oh, what a horrid brood it can count as its offspring! Oaths and curses, blasphemies and affronts, reproaches and injuries, can all point to it as their parent. Where is the slave of anger that is not likewise the slave of malice, hatred, and revenge? Is it not the prompter to bloodshed, the wicked inspirer of murder, and the occasion of untold scandal? Without peace, without health of soul, and often a prey to ill-health of body, is the unfortunate lot of persons controlled by this most pernicious vice. Pride and self-love are its secret springs, hence who could imagine a contrast greater than that which exists between a man the slave of such a complication of vice, and a disciple of Christ? It is like that of comparing a lamb to a tiger. We should not forget that, though some temperaments are more inclined to this vice than others, it can, if not corrected in time, grow uncontrollable in most people. Its pitiable sway over others it will have over us, if we be not faithful in the application of remedies. The dreadful future before us, if we allow this vice to control us, should be constantly before our minds. We will perceive it filled with the most gloomy forebodings from the side of our fellow-beings, as well as from the side of God. After a miserable life in which we will not have known peace, we will hear pronounced against us the awful sentence "depart from Me ye workers of iniquity." Behold what is in store for you, O angry, revengeful man! After convincing ourselves of the miseries in store for us, if we correct not this vice, we should turn ourselves to the earnest use of those remedies with which Christians resolving on becoming lives correct themselves of vice. They have been prescribed by Our Lord and are therefore of divine significance. We should, like the general of an army, who is liable to be attacked by the enemy at any time, be constantly watchful. Like a general, indifferent to this precaution, if we will neglect it, we will show that the cause of victory gives us little concern. Our watching will be to as little purpose as the general's, who should fool-like expect to withstand the attacks of the enemy without arms, if we fail to unite fervent prayer to our watching. Our Lord united them in the prescription: "Watch ye and pray, lest ye enter into temptation." Who is there that has experienced the little purpose to which he made resolutions to correct himself of his vice, so long as he depended on his own strength, and does not realize the absolute need of aid from Heaven to insure success? Prayer is the means which Our Lord tells us to use that this aid may be forthcoming. But like the general who will have watched and provided himself with the necessary arms, but fails disastrously to use them, or at least to the best possible advantage, and is therefore conquered, unless in all the attacks of the enemy we use prayer, and to the best possible advantage, or in other words, unless we fight like true Christians with this God-given means, we will not be crowned with victory. Every poor, vice-ridden Christian is a coward. Besides, to be successful in eradicating this vice, the volume of our lives revealing all the sins and shortcomings of the past, especially such as we may have been plunged into by anger, must by frequent reflection become familiar to us. This study will aim a death blow at that pride which is ever prominent in slaves of anger. If this were not so, how could they be so captious, so sensitive; why should they swell with indignation, fly at those who oppose or contradict them, and thirst for revenge? Whatever then, as is clear, will tend to disabuse us of that pernicious overrating of ourselves, will prove of great utility in overcoming anger. The more insignificant to ourselves we become, the less pride will be in us and, by consequence, the easier it would be to conquer the vice of anger. Who that is little in his own eyes; who that esteems himself mean and despicable, and asks to be no better in the estimation of others, will be quick to anger? And yet, though it may seem of a caste too exalted for ordinary Christians, this is but the spirit which actuates the genuine disciple of the humble and meek Jesus. Ah, dear people, our conceit is the curse that begets all our ills, not the least of which is anger. Let us divest ourselves of conceit by the acquirement of a correct knowledge of ourselves, and we will not have the excesses into which anger plunges us, to deplore. If our lives have been sadly tarnished with angry extremes, it has been because we have deceived ourselves, by closing our eyes to all the dark pictures of the past, and opening them but to view whatever flattered our pride or vanity. If now, at last, we seriously desire to stamp out the vice of anger, we must reverse the order by keeping our eyes wide open to aught that will humble us, and scrupulously closed to whatever might tend to fan pride or vanity.

In this short discourse sufficient has been said to give us some notion of how we are to rid or guard ourselves from the vice of anger and its horrid offspring. The means of eradication are most simple, and conveniently within the reach of all. If a bright, cheerful, and happy future be our selection, then henceforth we will call them into use, but if a future similar to the lives of slaves of anger and an eternity of misery be our choice, then no means need be used to correct or protect us from this vice.

XXIII.

FIFTH SUNDAY AFTER EASTER.

"Be ye doers of the word, and not hearers only, deceiving your own selves."—James i. 22.

The obligation which Catholics have to hear the word of God, in sermons and instructions, is not satisfied, save by those who not only hear it but keep it to regulate their lives. Not the hearers, but those who hear and keep His word did Our Lord pronounce blessed. Those who reap no good fruit from sermons and instructions are like the pharisees in so far that they hear them not with a view to their betterment. They who have a cause at heart value every word said to promote their success; this is the motive which actuates every earnest Christian in hearing God's word. Evident, then it is, why so few of every congregation return to their homes any the better of what had been said. Shall it be well with those who thus abuse this God-given talent? Ah, no; for the arm of God's justice is not shortened. The God that the pharisees thus provoked is the God whom they provoke, and as those were given up to their hardness of heart. Christians of to-day, who imitate them in their abuse of one of Heaven's best gifts, are likely to fare no better. A most wholesome disposition, therefore, which every Christian should have in hearing sermons and instructions, is that of fear, lest in the event of his not reaping actual fruit from those divine messages, God might deal with him as He had with so many thousands who had heard and heeded not. What a blessing it would be if all who hear sermons and instructions would not be slow to allow this wholesome fear of God to penetrate their hearts. Then indeed, so many who have heard, but in vain, sufficient to convert a nation well disposed, would not, living and dying, be cursed with bitter hardness of heart.

The reasons for this deplorable barrenness of soul of those who hear God's word without fruit, are manifold. Some of them are totally devoid of religious feeling, and listen to a sermon or an instruction by way of pastime, as they would to a rostrum speaker on a very indifferent subject. Their interest is so very defective that, let the speaker be ever so entertaining and clear in his diction, on leaving the church they are scarcely able to mention a brace of ideas of the sermon. The truth is that during the sermon they are the willing victims of thoughts foreign to the occasion. Some have their minds on business, others on pleasures; in a word, their minds are open to anything that presents itself, save what the priest utters. Such people, it is needless to say, might pretend during their whole lives to be passing good hearers of the most striking and penetrating sermons, without fruit to their souls, or Christian rules to their manner of living. Others there are who to some extent are affected by what is said, and resolve, in a half-hearted way, to make needed corrections in their lives, but, save slight moves, they stop there. The surroundings of their waywardness have too great a hold on them, and the effects of the sermon are soon lost. Oh, this is one of the great reasons why so few young persons, especially who really hear sermons and are moved by them, become true, persevering converts. If they would but allow the good impressions to take root in their souls by absenting themselves from whatever or whoever tends to lessen the spirit of religion in their souls, their conversion would be a certainty. But so long as they remain or put themselves in dangerous circumstances, all the fruit of all they hear will be lost. Besides these we have considered, there is, in almost every congregation, a number of the more sedate and apparently sensible people of the parish, who pay strict and respectful attention to what is said, and carry away an intelligent account of the sermon with concomitant impressions capable of yielding much fruit, but, alas! their engrossing worldly solicitude proves a killing blight to the best impressions, and they die short of fruit. Week after week this predominance of material things over matters spiritual is sadly repeated in them, so that they live benumbed to religion because of their grasping, engrossing worldliness. As Our Lord expressed it, they are engrosed " with the cares and riches and pleasures of this life, and yield no fruit." They have not yet learned the lesson taught by Our Lord: " Seek first the kingdom of God, and all these things shall be added." They yet put more confidence in themselves than in God, and in doing so " they catch at the shadow and lose the substance." Who can be found, true to the cause of God and his own salvation, that wants for sustenance? "I have not seen the just forsaken, nor his seed begging their bread." " Cast thy care upon the Lord and He shall sustain thee." Hence all who will disabuse themselves of that engrossing solicitude which interferes with their service of God, and confide in Him, will not be forsaken, and will not even, as we learn from the sacred scriptures, want things temporal.

Can not people practice what is preached and fill faithfully their respective stations in life? Is a man less capable of serving his purpose in the affairs of life because he is religiously devout? In heaven there are Saints from all respectable stations in life. Because whilst on earth they aimed to be Saints, were they therefore less qualified for their duties as men of affairs? Doubtless the record of their lives would not show that they were. They looked upon those duties as a part of the service which they owed to God, hence they attended to them with conscientious fidelity. But they allowed not the abuse to enter into their lives, which is, alas! only too common, of foregoing purely spiritual duties to give exclusive attention to the common affairs of life. In this rests the difference between those who practise not what they hear in sermons and instructions, and those who hear to put in practice. The latter, sad to say, is a small minority of every congregation. Of the number that listen to me now, only the very few will derive the practical fruit from what I say, which God desires all should gain. By far the greater number will as fruitlessly listen to sermons and instructions in the future as if no word of admonition as to how they should profit by God's word was ever uttered in their hearing. So is it with regard to every other abuse to which some people are especially prone; each person can from time to time hear his case pictured, and listen to the strongest motives urging him to correct himself; the means, too, will be mentioned by which he can effect the change, and yet the vast majority will continue to live as if they had heard not a word. The religiously indifferent man remains as he has been; the profaner still continues his vile traffic of the sacred names of the Deity; the unjust repents not, and by consequence restores not, though each has heard his case set forth in the strongest light with all the terrible consequences that must come if a change be not effected. Have I not before me, whilst I speak, some who have continued to offend God by the commission of certain vices, notwithstanding that they have frequently heard the most powerful sermons against their favorite vices, picturing the dreadful ruin that awaits them unless they cease and repent? May God pity them! Fearful in the extreme is their condition; it bespeaks a hardness of heart that every sane man should dread.

We see, dear people, how very dangerous it is to abuse this gift of God, by hearing sermons and instructions unfruitfully. We should allow a wholesome fear of God to deter us from that which has cost so many the dread calamity of utter hardness of heart and final impenitence—a repetition in their regard of what befell the inhabitants of the cities of old that hardened their hearts against God's word.

XXIV.

SIXTH SUNDAY AFTER EASTER.

HOW THE FRIENDS AND ENEMIES OF THE HOLY GHOST WILL FARE ON PENTECOST.

"Be prudent, and watch in prayers."—1 Peter iv. 1.

The apostle but repeats in this short sentence precepts of our Blessed Lord. At all times it is our duty as Christians to practise them, but since it is to be hoped that all who have respect for the voice of their Mother the Church, and regard for the safety of their souls, have made their peace with God by a good Easter Confession, the time intervening the fulfilment of that sacred and fruitful duty and the coming of the Holy Ghost, furnishes a reason why they should more particularly practise those virtues. What better means could they make use of to preserve that peace; what more effectual way could they prepare themselves for the reception of the Holy Ghost and His blessed gifts, than the practise of the virtues mentioned by Saint Peter? You need not be informed that the Holy Ghost will not enter a soul that has not the peace of a good conscience, nor need you be told that they who recently acquired this peace in the reception of the Sacrament of Penance, can easily forfeit it again if they be not prudent, watchful, and prayerful. By a more devoted practice of these virtues in this particular time, they will so dispose themselves as to receive greater strength from the Holy Ghost, to execute the resolutions which they took on the day of their repentance. Clear then is the need which those who have resolved upon a new life for the future have to hearken to the admonitions of the apostle. They must certainly be convinced, from the sad experience of that past for which they must now grieve, that they cannot hope to persevere if they rely on their own strength, and they cannot expect to receive aid from God unless they obey His requests. In the words of His apostle, He tells them as His divine Son had told them, to be prudent in avoiding those associations and places which proved to them to be the sad occasions of those sins which they must henceforth deplore; to be constantly on the watch for dangers, both from within and without, and in holy prayer, embracing all the conditions rendering it acceptable to Him, to sue most earnestly for His divine aid.

But as those who stand and have always stood firm in the service of God and the cause of their salvation, should fear, lest they might fall, they too have in this wholesome fear a powerful reason urging them to the practice more seduously in this particular time, prudence, watchfulness, and prayer. They should convince themselves that since not to receive becomingly or utilize fully the gifts of God, is to displease Him, their fidelity in the practice of those virtues should, in preparation for the feast of Pentecost, attain its full measure. They should not forget that every move which they make in honor of the Holy Spirit will be most amply rewarded on the day of Pentecost. Oh, what treasures of divine favors the Holy Ghost will bestow on those who will by prudence, watchfulness, and prayer, prepare themselves to celebrate, with ardent Christian devotion, the great anniversary of His visible descent to be the Soul, the Inspirer and Guide of the Church for all time! They can well expect to experience additional zeal and vigor in the service of God and the cause of their salvation. In proportion to our preparation will be our dispositions, and the latter will bespeak the extent of the favors which we can expect. Some, because of their worthy dispositions, will abound in new spiritual favors on that day; others less worthy, for they will be found to have taken less pains to prepare, whilst they will be rewarded according to their merits, will not so abound; and others again will be little the better of that hallowed day on account of their lack of preparation. But the sad picture is that of those of every parish who will be even the worse for that day. Yes, dear people, in this as in every other parish will there be Catholics who, on the blessed day of Pentecost, will greatly disgust high Heaven with the filth of their souls. They will on that day, sad to say, of their own free volition, be infested by as many evil spirits as they will possess ungovernable passions. In their souls, of course, the Holy Ghost will have no place, nor will they have any share in His gifts. That day, so rich in divine favors for others, will prove for them another crying abuse of God's great gifts to man. Are there those here whose consciences upbraid them with the guilt of mortal sin? Such they are, if they will so continue, as will abuse that sacred day: So deplorably devoid of prudence are they that in the sad state of damnation they walk on the very brink of hell, liable at any moment to tumble headlong into that awful abyss, where they must remain forever the prey of torments which rival in the contrary extreme the bliss of heaven; so devoid of watchfulness are they that they recklessly throw themselves into arms of vice, irrespective of consequences; and so little regard have they for all divine succor that they never utter a prayer. Oh, what a sad condition for Catholics, who vowed before God's altar, in the most solemn manner, to be faithful Christians! On that sacred day, whilst the Holy Spirit will communicate to souls prepared to receive His blessed gifts, a very foretaste of the happiness of heaven, those miserable people must taste of the bitterness of hell in the remorse of a guilty conscience. What, O men! who thus groan under the pangs of a guilty conscience, do you intend? Will you continue the prey of the hellish brood of foul spirits that now possess you, rather than by a good confession to expel them and give place to the Holy Spirit? Ah, I beg of you, be prudent, be watchful, be prayerful for once in your life; drive from you those wicked spirits that seek your ruin, and prepare your much persecuted poor souls to receive the Holy Ghost, the Comforter, who desires your eternal happiness. But not those only who are open violators of the laws of God and the Church, will deprive themselves of the blessings of Pentecost. There is a class of persons who make some pretensions of being actuated by the Spirit of God, whilst in truth the spirit of the world holds control. They too, since shallow pretense is worth nothing before God, will deprive themselves of the rich favors of Pentecost. "We," says the apostle, "have received not the spirit of the world, but the Spirit that is of God, the Paraclete, the Spirit of truth, whom the world cannot receive." We have it from the divine lips of Our Lord that God and the world we cannot simultaneously love; neither can we be actuated at the same time by the spirit of the world and the Spirit of God. The whole heart, the whole soul must be given to God, otherwise, since the Spirit of God will not keep company with the spirit of the world, we cannot expect to have part with those who will profit by Pentecost. Prudence, as recommended by the apostle, should suggest to us to examine ourselves, so as to be sure that no trace of the world's spirit finds place in us. If pride and vanity betray themselves; if a secret selfishness and attachment to the world and its goods are traceable in us; if disorderly affections carry us about in their whims, it is clear that we too shall be shut out from the favors of the Holy Ghost, though we may appear passing good Christians. These are signs that the spirit of the world sways us, and till we rid ourselves of it, we cannot hope that the Holy Spirit will take up His abode in our souls. Oh, how numerous are those who shut out the Spirit of God from their souls in this way, whilst they pass as good Christians before men! They are neither prudent, nor watchful, nor prayerful, in the sense of the apostle.

Then, dear people, as you must perceive, to practice the virtues of our text in the manner that the present season demands, we must not only be free from mortal sin, and all affection thereto, but we must likewise be prepared to give up to the Holy Spirit our whole heart and soul, for on this condition only will He abide with us.

XXV.
PENTECOST.

"But tho Paraclete, the Holy Ghost, whom the Father will send in my name, He will teach you all things, and bring all things to your mind, whatsoever I shall have said to you."—John xiv. 26.

It should be a matter of grave concern with all of us to-day to be able to feel satisfied that the Holy Ghost abides within us individually. Should the contrary be our unfortunate plight, our participation in the celebration of this the anniversary of His visible coming, to be the Soul and Guide of the Church, and the Soul and Comforter of the souls of God-fearing people, would be but a mockery. We cannot do Him honor so long as we continue to do Him the gravest injustice by depriving Him of occupancy of His spiritual temple within us. No one here need be told that mortal sin and the Holy Ghost cannot abide in the soul at the same time; nor should it be necessary to say that, for want of dispositions, some only pretend to repent of their sins. If there be one here who is conscious of a mortal sin for which he has not repented, or if there be one here who lacked sorrow for having offended God, hatred for his sins, a firm purpose of amendment, with a will to make satisfaction to God in his seeming repentence, we, alas! have in our midst, one who honors not the Holy Ghost, one who is guilty of the most grave injustice towards the Holy Ghost. Unless such a one resolve to-day to change from his sad condition, this day, full of consolation for all good Christians, will not only be without aught of consolation for him, but it will even rise up in judgment against him, as an abuse of an occasion of rich and numerous graces. In vain would we expect to find in the person whose soul is not occupied by the Holy Ghost, true Christian earnestness, the offspring of zeal for his sanctification and salvation. Instead of a firm, lively faith, his daily life will give evidence of a faith that is dull and even quite dead. The condition of his hope is in line with that of his faith, as his insensibility of eternal truths and want of esteem for spiritual matters but too well betray. What can such a person show in his daily life worthy of a Christian? What virtues does he practise; what vices does he avoid because of his love of God and man? Ah, dear people, when the Holy Ghost is not in the soul of a man, there need be no question of finding either positive or negative supernatural virtue in him. And a man's interior sentiments expressed in words, and the tenor of his every-day private life, furnish the best means to arrive at a correct judgment as to the presence or non-presence of that Divine Guest.

But when the Holy Ghost abides in the soul of a man, he is fully alive to the grave importance of all eternal truths, and to the consummate value of the means destined to enable him to conform his life to the grave demands of these truths. Enlightened by the Holy Spirit dwelling within him, he lives fully convinced of the necessity of practising virtue, and of his own inability to do so without the every-day use of the ordinary Christian means. Thus enlightened, the value of prayer and spiritual reading, of every act of charity and worship, and of every positive and negative virtue practised, is fully estimated—" He will teach you all things, and bring all things to your mind whatsoever I shall have said to you." Not less will be the blessed effects of the indwelling of the Holy Ghost with regard to a man's judgment of sin. As man without the Holy Ghost, save in so far as it suits his self-respect or policy to be otherwise, is indifferent alike to virtue and vice, man possessed of the Divine Spirit is alive alike to the great value of virtue and of aught that would insure it to him, and of the enormity of the evil of sin. He is thoroughly convinced of the profit which accrues to him from the former, and of the loss that he sustains by the latter. This conviction and the grace which the Holy Ghost imparts to a man to live as it demands, are the grand effects of His indwelling in the soul, and form the vast difference between the sentiments and motives of action with regard to virtue and vice of those actuated by the Spirit of God, and the sentiments and motives of action with regard to virtue and vice of the many within and without the Church that are, unfortunately for themselves, religion, and society, possessed of a spirit quite other than the Holy Ghost. The greater the number possessed of the Holy Ghost, the smaller will be the number of those that depreciate virtue and appreciate vice in their hearts. The true way, therefore, to increase the reign of virtue and decrease that of vice among men, is to put forth our best efforts in our various capacities, to bring people under the blessed influence of the Holy Ghost. Whilst this is neglected, all vaunted reformatory moves must prove of no permanent value. Man must love virtue and hate vice before he can practise the one and abstain from the other. This he can never do, save when influenced by the Holy Ghost. Under His blessed influence, man becomes convinced of the enormity of sin, of the beauty of virtue, of the hallowed justice of Our Lord in commanding the avoiding of vice and practise of virtue, of the false judgment of the world in respect to virtue and vice, and of the rigorous judgment of God to be exercised to the full towards all those who will have lived in line with the false judgment of the world. From this divine influence come also the graces without which man's convictions in matters supernatural are never followed, " When He shall come, He will convince the world of sin, of justice and of judgment "—and furnish the graces to follow these convictions.

Thus we can form some idea of the great blessing of having the Holy Ghost in our souls. But we should not forget to use the means to preserve Him there. It certainly becomes our duty not to neglect the Divine Guest. He justly expects to be entertained, and will cease to be our Guest if we be wanting in this duty. If we desire Him to remain with us, we must be willing to remain with Him. The thought of His divine presence should often, in the course of the day, fill our hearts, and keep us on our guard never to introduce into our souls sentiments unfit to appear in His presence. Of our hearts, He is most jealous, and should we divide their affection between Him and creatures, He would cease to be our Guest. The whole heart of man He fashioned for Himself, and man's whole heart or none must He have. This is why so many are without Him in their souls. If self, if money, or any creature be loved inordinately, let us not deceive ourselves, the Holy Ghost is not in our souls. They are loved inordinately if they captivate our hearts, and to discover this is not difficult. When such is the case, they are idols set up in the temple of the Holy Ghost, and with such He will not dwell, be the objects in themselves ever so innocent. Or rather let us say in the sentiments of holy Church, "without the Holy Ghost there is nothing in man, there is nothing that is innocent." These idols are so many thieves that combine to rob man of his salvation, and the Holy Ghost of His temple. If man would imitate our Blessed Lord, which he must do or be a castaway, he should in the exercise of his free will handle the scourge to free his soul of them. But his duty ends not with this, for his soul should be a temple of prayer. Alas! how many there are in this parish even, to whom the Holy Ghost could say: "My temple is a temple of prayer, but you have made it a den of thieves."

Can we not, brethren, from these few thoughts, carry away with us some knowledge, at least, of the vast importance of having the Holy Ghost in our souls? Is it not He that makes all good, God-fearing people so bright and sensitive in everything pertaining to salvation, and so fearful of the evil of sin and tender-conscienced of aught savoring of it? Is it not the want of the Holy Ghost in men's souls that curses so many with that deplorable indifference to even the most terrible eternal truths; and with that disposition to make light of all vice, only in so far as self-respect or policy demand the contrary, which we see so common? Is it in line with the purpose of our existence and Christianity that we should be of those without the Holy Ghost? Ah, no; then let us be sure to-day that we are under the influence of the Holy Ghost, and let us never tire in the use of the means to keep under His blessed influence.

XXVI.
TRINITY SUNDAY.

"For of Him, and by Him, and in Him are all things; to Him be glory forever. Amen."—Romans. xi. 36.

A little less than six thousand years have rolled into the eternity of the past since the Almighty Triune God commenced time with His immortal fiat. Millions after millions of human beings have come, acted parts upon the world's stage, and gone forever out into the great hereafter. Whilst all these millions have been coming, acting, and going, who ever thought of us here to-day? Who of the vast multitude ever entertained a thought that we were even among the possible human beings that would some time people the earth? Ah, dear people, it is needless to say that all of them were as ignorant of our possibility and future existence, as we are of the possibility and future existence of those who will enter the world after we shall have gone. But whilst all these millions have been in profound ignorance of us, there has been one, the Triune God, who not only from the beginning of time, but throughout eternity, has never lost sight of us; nor will He in the eternity of the future. As possible beings, as real existing beings and as saved or lost beings we have always been and will always be, present to His adorable mind. He it was who in His divine economy raised us to the dignity of possible beings;

He it was who endowed us with the boon of existence; and He it is who has sustained that existence. All this He has done for a purpose worthy of Himself. He asks us not to believe other than Himself announcing His divine purpose. He tells us it is that we may be His servants in this world, and His courtiers in heaven. He has laid down the rules of this service which we exist to pursue, and He furnishes us with the means to fidelity. It is true, we have all been born children of wrath, and existence and preservation would avail us little, nay, would prove an eternal burden without that other still greater expression of His infinite generosity—redemption. This is the grand source whence the means come, which enable us to comply with those rules.

In this, as in our creation and preservation, the three persons of the most blessed Trinity participated—"When the fulness of time was come, God sent His Son, made of a woman." From this we see that God the Father participated so far in our redemption that He sent His divine Son to redeem man, in fulfilment of the promise made by the Triune God to the fallen parents of the human family four thousand years before. And our blessed Lord tells us that He came to do the will of His Father. Hence, whilst God the Son actually effected the great work of our redemption, He but did the will of God the Father. The redemption effected, God the Son sent God the Holy Ghost to apply its blessed fruits to the souls of men to the end of time. Without this application that great mystery of God's mercy would not avail us. So for our redemption, as well as for our creation and preservation, we owe an eternal debt of gratitude to God the

Father, God the Son, and God the Holy Ghost. The way to discharge this debt is to be faithful in God's service, for which we exist and are redeemed. Not only gratitude, but as what we have so far considered suffices to show, also justice obliges us to this service. Should we serve not God, we serve either the devil, the world, or the flesh, or better say all three. The Triune God made us, redeemed us, and sustains us for Himself. The soul that He has given to each of us He has qualified to know, love, and enjoy Him; and she is so constituted that true peace or happiness she cannot have if torn from His service. This is the great cause of the wretched want of peace and happiness, even among those upon whom the world has lavished its richest favors. It is needless to say that neither the devil, the world, nor the flesh had any part whatever in bestowing upon us the boons of creation, redemption, and conservation. On the contrary, their combined and constant aim is to ruin us for time and eternity. No proof is needed to convince us that this is the aim of the devil, nor is it necessary to advance arguments to show that the world is constantly tempting men to abandon God's service. But of all, our most dangerous enemy is our own flesh. Is it possible to imagine a more inveterate enemy than one who is satisfied to bring ruin upon himself, if in doing so he can effect the ruin of another? Thus man's flesh bears itself towards his soul; it aims to eternally ruin his soul, though the ruin of the latter means the ruin of both. The man, therefore, who serves not his God, serves these enemies of God and self, and in doing so, robs God of what is due Him by the strongest titles. Besides the absolute titles at which we have but hinted, there remains another in our case, since we are Christians, too important to be overlooked. Have we not been consecrated to the most blessed Trinity? At the foot of God's altar each one of us solemnly entered into a covenant with the Trinity, binding himself to the Triune God's service. On the strength of this covenant he was admitted into that "one fold" established by Christ, and the act of admission was none other than his consecration to the Father, the Son, and the Holy Ghost. How do we look upon the action of those who put to profane uses what once had been consecrated to the service of God? Do we not brand this work, and truly too, a sacrilege? Of this every Christian is guilty who turns from the service of the Triune God, and gives himself to the service of the devil, the world, and the flesh. So no matter how we view ourselves, we are confronted with the truth that we belong to the Triune God, and whenever we do aught not conformable to this, we depart from the end of our existence, the end of our conservation, the end of our redemption, and the end of our Christian consecration, and therefore sin.

If we would live aright in the midst of enemies whose aim is to cheat us of our salvation, we have but one line to follow. That has been marked out for us by the blessed example and doctrine of Our Lord. All the God-fearing Christian men and women that have lived upon this earth have followed the line of conduct thus traced out.

This we must likewise do if we would answer to the end of our existence, the end of our redemption, the end of our consecration, by our fidelity in the service of the Triune God. "I came down from heaven, not to do My own will, but the will of Him that sent

Me." This is, as we have seen, the precise reason for which the Triune God sent each one of us into the world. We are here not to do as we please, but as He pleases, for we belong not to ourselves, but to Him. He has not made us slaves, but free beings, fully qualified, if we will, to know that this is our duty. What Our Lord said of Himself: "My meat is to do the will of Him that sent Me," contains a lesson that has been well learned by all truly God-fearing people, and must be by us, if we would take our place among them in eternity. All of us know the Triune God's will in our regard. Besides what His will exacts from us in the discharge of our Christian duties, each has the duties of his station in life, which must always be fulfilled in keeping with God's good pleasure. It is needless to remark that the king in his palace, as well as the peasant in his hut, is obliged to thus serve the Triune God, the King of kings; and if he fail, his crown will not save him from damnation, for "God is not a respecter of persons." As we advance in age, we should grow in virtue. Our blessed Model, though always infinite in wisdom and grace, was pleased, as man, for our instruction, to show by degrees as He advanced in age, His wisdom and grace. "Jesus advanced in wisdom and age and grace with God and man." If we be faithful to our common Christian duties; if we discharge in a Christian spirit those of our respective stations in life, we will daily become better fortified by grace, and by consequence better able to cope with difficulties, and make greater strides in virtue.

Let each apply, as directed, to himself these few thoughts, and let him see whether or not he is true to the end of his existence and Christianity, serving the

Triune God. If he be compelled to admit that he is not, let him honor the most blessed Trinity by a heartfelt resolution to begin a new life.

XXVII.

SECOND SUNDAY AFTER PENTECOST.

" Wonder not, if the world hate you."—1 John iii. 13.

It should indeed be no occasion of wonder to the thoughtful Christian that the world to which the Apostle refers, regards with hatred the true followers of our blessed Lord. Has not Our Lord pronounced the archenemy of God and man the "prince of this world?" What could be expected then, save that the spirit and maxims of the world should be diametrically opposite to those of Christianity! Is there a single tenet of Christianity which the world has not called in question, ignored, and ridiculed? And this too, by placing man above God in presuming to improve, refine, and elevate the Christianity of Christ. Whilst it dislikes to give up the Christian name, because it is a synonym for civilization, the world repudiates Christ-given Christianity, for its incompatibility with human pride and kindred passions. The Christianity of Christ and of His true followers the world even hates because of its antagonism to "the lust of the flesh, the lust of the eyes, and the pride of life" with which the same Apostle tells us it abounds. Should it be an occasion of wonder then that the world hates Christ and His true followers?

Clear then is the attitude of the world with regard to true Christian principles and their faithful professors. To be consistent, our disposition with regard to the spirit and maxims of the world should not be less clear. Our Lord has declared against the world in the most pronounced manner, so that if the world's spirit and maxims find place in us, we know where we stand. His spirit, His maxims, will not keep company with those of the world, hence to be possessed of them, we must be fully divested of the world's. Ah, how often is it the case that the children of the household of the faith are as great strangers to the spirit and maxims of Christ as those from whom we could scarcely expect better! How often do we in common with those who have declared against Christ, find them worshipping at the shrines of the three great gods of the world, unlawful pleasures, honors purchased at the sacrifice of conscience, and ill-gotten riches! Can a man possessed of living faith experience contentment in this role? For me it is impossible to understand how he can, and yet without contentment, without peace of conscience, a man's life is a very hell upon earth. Oh, that men would suffer one-tenth for virtue's sake that they bow to in the commission of vice, what rich crowns would be their recompense! If men who thus throw all that is most dear to them away for vanities that ere long will be torn from them, ever in their lives experienced the contentment, the real happiness of a good conscience, which is the exclusive portion of faithful servants of God, they must in their thoughtful moments sorely feel their deplorable exchange. A life of misery like theirs with a very probable terrible eternity before them, to my mind, and to any reasonable man's mind, is an enormous price to give for what this world holds out. Every age has had its fools within the Christian ranks, and is likely to have them to the end of time; and I may add that there are few parishes without specimens of rank foolishness of this kind. So long as persons live by the principles and are actuated by the spirit of the world, be their pretensions to a Christian life what they may, they are not followers of Christ, but slaves to that world against which Our Lord has declared. How could a slave to unlawful sensual pleasures; how could one who has purchased honors by tricks and schemes in no way in keeping with the spirit and maxims of Christianity; how, in fine, could a man who takes advantage of opportunities to defraud his neighbor, be reckoned among good conscientious Christian people? He may show himself among the congregation; he may contribute towards the maintenance of the Church; but in the full sense of the term he is not a Catholic. As well as being a member of the body of the Church, he must belong to her soul to be in the strict sense a Catholic. This he can never be so long as for the sake of pleasures, or honors, or riches, he fails to respect and obey her precepts and the commandments of God. True followers of Our Lord, or in other words, true, earnest Catholics, are counted at the communion railing, and here it is needless to say we fail to find men actuated with the world's spirit and guided by its maxims. Nothing can be more different than the spirit and maxims of the world, and those of Our Lord. Whilst the former degrade man by turning him from the end of his existence, the blessed example and teaching of Our Lord ennobles, spiritualizes, and carries forward to that better life, for which they were created and redeemed, all who wish to be His disciples. Self-gratification and indulgence, irrespective of the laws of God and His Church, are the want of the world's votaries; whilst the aim of the true follower of Our Lord is to deny himself daily more and more. The world's slaves are willing to suffer all manner of trials and dangers in the commission of vice, but they laugh at the idea of bearing aught for the sake of virtue, or for the honor and glory of God, nay, in trials they rage, profane, and not unfrequently blaspheme. But the good, earnest Christian not only bears with religious resignation the crosses which God is pleased to send him, but also in a spirit of mortification imposes others upon himself. It is unnecessary to proceed further to arrive at the conclusion that, since the ways of worldings are so different from those of the true earnest followers of Our blessed Lord, that a mutual hatred exists for each other's ways. The more, therefore, our manner of living is in opposition to the spirit and maxims of the world, the more Christlike we have become. Our departure from the one and advancement in the other will be in proportion to our obedience in fulfilling the conditions laid down for all good Christians by Our Lord. They are contained in these words, which embrace the whole duty of the Christian: "If any man will come after Me, let him deny himself, and take up his cross, and follow Me." Fidelity in what is required of us in this sentence, will make us true haters of the spirit and maxims of the world, and true followers of Our Lord. Now, both the one and the other we must be, to save our souls. No one of a religious sense will deny the sad havoc that sin has made in poor human nature; no one who has any knowledge of the dreadful effects of sin on the creature, whether angel or man, will deny the seriousness of the wounds which sin has caused, and left in the faculties of his soul; nor is there any one who has even an imperfect knowledge of himself, prepared to deny that his passions and inclinations violently tend towards evil. Does not all this show the necessity we are under of denying ourselves in order to lead a Christian life? Our Lord has led the way, carrying His cross, and we must follow in His blessed footsteps. We must, as He tells us, "take up our cross." Some have heavier crosses than others to carry, but they have been distributed according to the good pleasure of God, and the heaviest is but the merest fragment of that of Our Lord. In proportion as fidelity in this common duty marked out for all appears in our daily lives, will we make ourselves the more hateful to the world, and the more lovable to Our Lord. Since from these few thoughts we can have some idea of the antagonism that exists between Our Lord and the world, and since we have long ago made choice of our side, it becomes us to be certain that we are on the side of the religiously sensible. Our examination of ourselves should be according to the conditions: "Deny thyself; take up thy cross and follow Me."

XXVIII.

THIRD SUNDAY AFTER PENTECOST.

"Casting all your care upon Him, for He hath care of you."—1 Pet. v. 7.

One of the chief duties of every Christian is to have a childlike confidence in God his Father. Any misgiving is unchristian and unjust, in so far as it detracts from the homage and adoration due to His divine majesty. Every thoughtful Christian is quite well aware that absolutely nothing can he do for the salvation of his soul without God. What a miserable plight then would be ours if there were any room to doubt God's fatherly care! So far from us having any warrant for diffidence, we are most strictly commanded by God to put our most implicit trust in Him—"Have confidence in the Lord with all thy heart, and do not lean upon thy own prudence." Clear then is the duty of every Christian in this matter; his whole heart must be consecrated to unstinted trust in God, coupled with the conviction of his own utter helplessness without aid from his heavenly Father. What have we that did not come from God, and what is there for which we hope that will prove of utility to us, that will not come from Him? All that we can count as our own are our sins, which we should deplore. Who then does not see that it would be stupid to diffide in God, and confide in self; and that his best interests call for his full trust in Him who has so favored him in the past, and pledges Himself to continue His fatherly care in the future? The Christian who corresponds with his duty as a child of the Church, "trusting perfectly in the grace which is offered him at the revelation of Jesus Christ," is preparing to receive the everlasting reward which God bestows upon His faithful servants. The reward of confidence in God is no less a boon than salvation—"We are," as the Scriptures tell us, "saved by hope." So that in the language of the Scriptures we may say: "Blessed are all they that trust in God." Millions after millions of the human family have, generation after generation, passed from earth into eternity, and we have God's word for it that not one who had trusted in Him ever suffered disappointment. The Christian who does his duty and confides in God like a prolific tree, always abounds in good fruit; his soul is constantly refreshed with the divine springs of grace, and as in a rich garden which suffers neither from heat nor drought, the flowers of virtue therein attain the highest perfection. From all this we can understand the extent of the injury which the Christian is guilty of towards God, by any want of confidence in His fatherly protection. He insults God by mistrusting His word, and he dishonors Him in his own soul by depriving her of the spiritual favors which confidence would insure to her. Is it any wonder then that we find in the Sacred Scriptures most awful threats against all those who lack confidence in God? It should be the constant aim of every Christian to bring upon himself the blessing of God, for thus only can he enjoy that interior peace without which life is a burden and an utter failure. From the moment that diffidence in God finds place in him he deplorably departs from this aim, and disposes himself for God's curse; and with this awful calamity will come hardness of heart, blindness to good, and a dryness and barrenness of soul terrible to contemplate. Oh, how often has the poor priest, burning with zeal for the salvation of every soul, to bring his best efforts to the rescue of such souls, when every delay is dangerous! How often too is he heart-broken at his poor success! In reading the lives of the saints, we perceive that one of the most striking features of the beautiful example which they afford us, is their great childlike confidence in God. They are our models, and to imitate them, as far as our weakness will permit, confidence in God must be a strong point in our lives. David, after adverting to the miseries which had befallen all who had not trusted in God, concluded by saying: "But it is good for me to stick close to my God—to put my hope in the Lord God." And holy Job cries out: "Although He should kill me, I will trust in Him." This unwavering confidence in God, so remarkable in David and Job, was no less strong in the other saintly men of the old law; but to speak of a saint of the new law is to bring before our minds a Christian with the utmost trust in God. In God's unlimited power, in His infinite goodness, and in His most rigorous fidelity to His promises, the saints have ever seen the most absolute exclusion of all possibility of their disappointment. This is just how we must always view the matter, and keep scrupulously clear of the slightest misgivings, no matter how great or how numerous the occasions may be which tend to shake our confidence in God.

No doubt the consideration of the number and malice of their past moral deformities, the black ingratitude of which they have been guilty towards God, and their utter unworthiness, would have the effect to drive some truly religious souls to desperation had they not in mind God's goodness and His infinite fidelity to His promises. Unworthy indeed we all are to be even thought of by God, but we should not forget that, whilst this is undoubtedly so, we have an infinitely worthy friend in our blessed Lord, who has most generously taken our part. Where, O Christian! is there any room for diffidence, or why should you have less than the fullest confidence, even though your sins were as numerous as the seconds in your life, and as black and offensive as the evil spirit that prompted their commission, since you have this divine Friend to turn to, who will receive you with all the tenderness of His infinite compassion? The reception of the prodigal by an affectionate father, who because of his love forgot the faults of his returning son, is but an imperfect figure of the expressions of love tendered the returning sinner by the Sacred Heart of Jesus. Who can think of His divine tenderness to Magdalen and the penitent on the cross, and have the least misgiving? In the Christian's vocabulary there can be no room for diffidence in this divine Benefactor. Whilst we were His enemies, God the Father sent His divine Son to die for us; whilst we were His enemies, our loving Jesus suffered unto death for us, and the Holy Ghost entered our souls and changed us from enemies to friends. Where then, O Christian, is the basis for diffidence? Has Christ not given power to His priests to absolve from sin; has He not given this power without limit, as to the number or gravity of the sins over which it is to be exercised? How then can any healthy-minded

Catholic have any misgivings? Let the Christian's distrust ever be in himself; let him be always mindful that of himself, absolutely nothing for his salvation can he do; but let him never forget that with God's grace nothing which will contribute to attaining the happy end of his existence can be impossible to him. This grace he will have for the mere asking, and with it he has no reason to fear that the dispositions will be wanting to him for the valid exercise in his case, of the Christ-given power in the priest. Oh, how grateful we should be to the good God who has dealt so mercifully and liberally with us poor creatures! It is the Christian's own fault if he be without Christ-given peace, for whatever may be his plight, he has but to reach for peace to have it. No matter how he may be tried; no matter to what extent he is tempted, and no matter how reckless may have been his past, which he heartily deplores, he has but to do the little required of him as a child of the Church, and confide in his infinitely loving Father, God, and his peace is assured.

Let us then, dear people, do our duty as humble Christians, and trust to God for a happy outcome. Away then, with all those unnecessary anxieties and scruples! They are but temptations to draw us from that childlike confidence which we should have in our heavenly Father. He is infinitely more desirous of our well-being, both here and hereafter, than we can be. How can we fail to confide in Him who sacrificed His eternal Son for our sake? Why should we not, every day of our lives, obey the voice of the Apostle, telling us "to cast our care upon Him, for He hath care of us?"

XXIX.
FOURTH SUNDAY AFTER PENTECOST.

"The sufferings of this time are not worthy to be compared with the glory to come, that shall be revealed in us."—Rom. viii. 18.

Besides God's word in the sacred scriptures expounded by His Church, the infallible interpreter which He has given us, we have the practical lives of His Saints, leading us to the conviction that all which man can suffer in this world in the cause of his salvation, is far less in its relative value to the reward than the most trifling piece of money would be to a kingdom, having within its vast compass the entire world. When viewed in the light of God the human suffering in the few years of this life,.compared with the least ray of consolation lasting forever, dwindles into insignificance. But aided by the same light on contemplating the sum of everlasting bliss, as is taught by Revelation, which God has prepared for all who love Him unto their death, all the sufferings of this life must appear to us as they did to the Saints—unworthy of consideration. Sufferings for righteous sake are always accompanied with the honey of a divine unction, which to a large extent robs them of their bitterness, whilst the bliss of heaven throughout eternity will experience no diminution. Time and eternity admit of no comparison; the same must be said of what ends with a very short span of time, as considered in relation to that which must last forever. Hence the words of the Apostle: "The sufferings of this time are not worthy to be compared with the glory to come." What the human body is capable of suffering is in no way comparable to what the immortal soul is capable of desiring. Easy indeed is it to exhaust the endurance of the bodies of most men, but it takes God Himself to satisfy the cravings of their souls. These are fully requited in the joys of the life to come. Revelation informs us that: "The eye hath not seen, nor the ear heard, neither hath it entered into the heart of man what things God hath prepared for them that love Him." When, after duly weighing the consoling meaning of this sentence, we give our thoughts to the sufferings of the Saints which have been undergone with the view to attain this glorious reward, we will have some conception of the infinite disparity between all that man can do and suffer on earth, and the indemnity in store for him in heaven. How marvellously grand, how strikingly beautiful, how contributive to earthly pleasure have been the scenes which the human eye has scanned! What is there truly admirable; what is there charming; what is there electrifying within the limit of human understanding that the most eloquent tongues have not described, in language inspired by passion's most lofty flights? And then the height, the depth, the breadth of human conception, and the power of man's imagination; how wonderful they are! Yet, all—all fall infinitely short of reaching the grandeur, the beauty, the perfection of the sum of delights which God has prepared for those who leave this exile in love with Him. In a word, what God has prepared for our future happiness is no less than infinite, for less could not satisfy the immortal soul of man—it is therefore God Himself.

Well have the Saints understood this; well too have they perceived the infinite disparity between all that man can do and suffer to gain heaven, and the happiness which shall there be his recompense. If we will be taught aright in this all-important matter, we must learn from them whose works have expressed their convictions, and not, as too many Catholics do, from the foolish children of this world, who are unstinted in their sacrifices for things earthly, but unwilling to do or suffer aught for the joys of God's everlasting kingdom. The Saints have disposed themselves by means of the light from on high, without which it is impossible to discern the things of God. "But we have received not the spirit of the world, but the spirit which is of God, that we might know the things that are given unto us by God." These then are the instructors from whose blessed lives we should inform ourselves how amazingly cheap heaven will be, when we attain it by doing and suffering all that the providence of God assigns us. They have formed their estimate of the happiness of heaven with minds illumined by light from above, and the works of their lives tell us that they have beheld unlimited value in that object of all their aspirations. We have but to read the history of their lives to be convinced of this. Let us open the book where it informs us of the lives of those apostolic men who first sowed the seeds of Christianity in the hearts of men and nations. Did not their labors and sufferings surpass by all odds those of men engaged in any other cause? Had the world ever beheld a display of zeal and self-sacrifice on the part of man like unto theirs? Did hell's strongest legions; did earth's most wicked and mightiest powers; did labors and sufferings the most dire, cool their zeal; discourage and force them to relinquish the holy cause? Ah, no; their very lives passed with them as nothing compared to the object for which they labored, suffered, bled, and died. Their strength, both of body and soul, was staid with the wine of consolation, which came to them from the thought that they battled to get eternal possession for themselves and for as many others as they possibly could of the " celestial Jerusalem." Unworthy of consideration they deemed their sufferings, as in the light of God they gazed on that sublime city, the walls of which are raised with " precious stones," and its every gate "a rich pearl"; whose mansions are most artistically composed of " choicest jewels, " and streets paved with "transparent gold"; in whose midst flows a " crystal river," the source of which is at the throne of God, and upon whose banks are " trees of life," the taste of the fruit of which impart immortality. That city within whose walls are all joys without alloy, and which will see an "everlasting day," because its "sun is the Lamb, and the light that shines therein the glory of God"; where hunger and thirst are unknown; where the citizens are " crowned heads," whose "reign will be everlasting," and whose bodies are brighter than the sun and endowed with " ever-flourishing youth." This description of the inspired one of the Scriptures, expressed in figures embodying all that is rich and precious according to our present notions, as they well knew, and as all the Saints have known, left the object of their aspirations undescribed, but served to keep the divine fire within burning till their Christian heroism received its everlasting crown. On this glorious city of God, infinitely beyond all description, those galaxies of illustrious champions who have gained possession of it through "fire and water," constantly like the Apostolic men who preceded them, kept their eyes. This was the divine incentive which constrained, as it were, the thousands after thousands in the ages of persecutions, to run with an alacrity as if to scenes of pleasure, to racks and gibbets, to scourges and axes. Who can tell before the great judgment day the extent of the sufferings of those glorious champions in the cause which placed upon their brows immortal crowns? How little they valued their sufferings as they gazed in the divine light which shone in upon their souls, on the everlasting prize above! Can less be said of those men and women of every condition in life who have edified the people of every age, and shed lustre upon their mother, the Church, by the sanctity of their lives? I refer to those Saints who, instead of purchasing with their blood and lives, which were not demanded of them, the everlasting crown, paid most willingly their price for it, by sacrificing to God their wills and inclinations. Their gaze, like that of the martyrs, was constantly upon the divine object, and no self-sacrifice was considered great, because of the prize in sight, in God's house of many mansions.

Can we not see, dear people, from these thoughts, how very trifling all we can suffer in God's service is, compared with the reward which awaits us in the mansions above? Can we not also see how unchristian those murmurs and complaints are which sometimes escape us, instead of allowing our hearts to glow with gratitude to the good God, who exacts so litttle from us for so much? Let us henceforth, like the Saints, keep in sight the glorious recompense.

XXX.

FIFTH SUNDAY AFTER PENTECOST.

"Let him seek after peace, and pursue it."—1. Pet. iii. 11.

When our blessed Lord ascended the heights of Calvary, and shed His life-blood for mankind, He purchased for us peace in time and in eternity. He has deposited the consoling boon in the treasury of His bounty, whence it will be dispensed to all seekers. Not such as the world gives is this peace, but verily, such as only God can give to man. Its seat is in the soul, and it acts as a divine cordial, ministering consolation from within, whatever may be the circumstances without. Life's true sweetness is not known to the man who enjoys not the blessing of Christ-given peace. Oh, how many there are who have never tasted this Heaven-sent cordial, notwithstanding its infinite cost, and the comfort, more than earthly, it affords! They have never made a draft for it on God's bounty. Stranger still is the sad fact that no small number of our communion know it not, because their lives are at variance with the request of the Apostle: "Seek peace." Of all others they most feel its want, yet whilst within easy reach, without it they miserably plod life's weary journey.

Before I begin to describe them, you have in your minds the character of the Catholics to whom I refer. What they do and what they fail to do have already singled them out as the members of the parish who ignore the Church's discipline with a view to order. Where order is not we fail to find peace. Do we not perceive this to be so in civil communities? Has not peace departed from a city, a town, or a village, when the laws are disregarded? So, too, is it with man when his life is not regulated according to the laws of religion and morality. In him the blessed boon of peace, which Christ purchased for all men, is not to be found. A disregarder of all law, a murderer, an enemy to God and man has not peace, and cannot have it so long as he curses himself with a life so abhorrent. The Catholic who persists in the deliberate violation of the law of God and his Church, figures in all these horrid characters. Consult your reason and your faith, and you will see in a glance that this is not overdrawn. The man who makes light of God's law will not hesitate to violate the civil law, providing his whims demand it and he can do so with impunity. The man who is not true to his God is not likely to prove true to his fellow-man, only in so far as he is constrained. By what name then, if not law ignorer, are we to express the character of the man who, left to his free will, respects neither human, ecclesiastical, nor divine law? We designate the man a murderer who kills his neighbor's or his own body. The soul, as all know, is man's superior part, and therefore more valuable than his body. How then is his case before God who murders the soul of his neighbor by leading him into sin, and his own soul by the commission of mortal sin? Is it not that of a murderer? Did he not violate God's command : " Thou shalt not kill," when he banished the life of grace from his brother's and his own soul? Can the love of God be in the heart of such a man? To answer this let us call to mind the words of God: "If you love Me, keep My commandments." He keeps not God's commandments, and therefore he loves Him not, and where the love of God is not the love of the neighbor cannot be. Again, God's words we have: "He that is not with Me is against Me," and all who are against God are His enemies, and all who are the enemies of God cannot be true to their fellow-man—they want but a favorable opportunity to show this. There we have an outline of the character of a bad Catholic, and no more need be said to prove that the soul of such a one is a stranger to Christ-given peace. What a deplorable state of misery, which must end in eternal woe if pursued, for one who knows how to possess that peace within short limit! Why, O man! do you groan under the misery of a vice-ridden soul when it is so easy for you to have peace? Let God's word give the answer: "The carnal man receiveth not the things of the Spirit of God: for they are foolishness unto him; neither can he know them because they are spiritually discerned."

St. Paul speaks for all who seek peace, not in creatures, but in God its source, when he says: "But we have received not the spirit of the world, but the Spirit which is of God, that we might know the things that are given unto us by God." Those blessed with the spirit of God are they who live conformably to the law of God and the precepts of His Church. They only are the enjoyers of Christ-given peace, for they only are law-abiding; they only treat their souls as the queen, not the servant of their nature; and they only can be said to be in charity with God and man. In storm and in sunshine the precious gift abides within, ministering sweetness in the varied circumstances of their lives. "The yoke of Christ is sweet, and His burden light" to all those who have within them the "continual feast of a good conscience." All are thus blessed who are in the enjoyment of God's divine presence in their souls by grace, which is the necessary preparation to His enjoyment in glory in the life to come. He is our only true peace and comfort in life's weary journey here below, and He only can be the reward answering to the full all the yearnings and aspirations of our souls when the race of life is over. Without God the soul cannot but be devoid of peace, for God made her for Himself, and so constituted her that less than Himself could never afford her peace. The love of those whose souls enjoy the divine presence of God by grace is of a nature like unto that of the saints in heaven. Theirs, however, is thoroughly refined and pure, whilst, at best, man's love for his God, so long as he remains on earth, is not without, in a greater or less degree, earthly alloy. So, too, does the peace which His friends enjoy on earth resemble that of His confirmed friends in heaven. Though neither confirmed in grace nor in glory, they are blessed with a confidence in God's liberality and protection which nothing can shake, and with a hope for future happiness, such as those once possessed who are now to the full in its enjoyment. Can aught that the world affords to its most favored ones bear any resemblance to the peace and comfort thus accruing to the friends of God upon earth? Ah, no; for this is that Christ-given peace, such as the world can never give, and which is the exclusive portion of those who live virtuously. Whether the circumstances of the various stages of their lives are to nature agreeable or trying, God is their helper and they fear not. He never forsakes them in their sufferings, though to worldlings it may seem otherwise, but fully redeems His promise of "being always with them in tribulation." Nay, He enables the more fervent, and hence more favored, even to rejoice in their sufferings, as in the case of St. Paul who, in speaking of himself, says that not only even did he rejoice, but that he over-abounded with joy in all tribulation. This soaring above nature is what we perceive, in reading the Acts of the Apostles, to have been not alone the virtue of St. Paul, but that of all the Apostles—"They departed rejoicing from the council because they were thought worthy to suffer contumely for the name of Jesus." And the lives of the saints, of every age and condition of life, have been marked by the same glorious flights of virtue, to which they have been carried as a bird on the wing by the strengthening grace of Jesus Christ. Neither the Apostles nor the saints that have reached the blessed kingdom, for which all have been created, have had a monopoly of this grace; like heaven, it is for all who have the will to possess it. Since by it, then, they have been carried forward to degrees of virtue which edified not only their contemporaries, but all future generations, and finally placed upon their brows the crowns which they now wear, why should we not at least edify those around us, and in the end reach our crowns above by the same grace? Let us have the will, and the rest will be accomplished by Him who wrought the wonders in them. Peace here and an eternal peace hereafter should be the motto of our lives.

XXXI.

SIXTH SUNDAY AFTER PENTECOST.

"We all, who are baptized in Christ Jesus, are baptized in His death."—Rom. vi. 8.

No one here need be reminded of the all-importance of the Sacrament of Baptism. All are well aware that the spiritual birth by " water and the Holy Ghost," in Baptism, is as absolutely necessary to attain the dignity of a Christian and a child of the Church, to qualify for the reception of the other Sacraments, and finally enter heaven, as the carnal birth is to enter the world and be numbered as one of the human kind. Nor is it necessary to say in the hearing of those present that when actual Baptism is not possible, the baptism of blood or desire would have the effect, regarding original and actual sin, that perfect contrition would have in respect to actual sin in the event of imminent death, should Sacramental Confession be out of the power of the person. What should receive our thoughts to-day is the solemn engagement which we entered into with God at our spiritual birth. In the death of our blessed Saviour, as the Apostle says in our text, " we are baptized." He died that we should be spiritually born. Have we ever taken the trouble to rightly understand all this, as well as the obligation which we then contracted?

The most precious blood of our dear Lord, shed on seven different occasions, the last of which was when His most Sacred Heart poured forth its hallowed contents, gives to the water and the words of Baptism their supernatural power of cleansing and sanctifying. When ushered into the world, the mark of the slave is upon the human soul; Heaven frowns upon it, and the sentence of eternal exclusion from the kingdom of its preordination is in line with its condition. The blood of our loving Jesus flowed for every soul, and Baptism is the first and most necessary means of applying its redeeming fruits thereto. In this Sacrament the mark of the slave of Satan gives place to the sacred and indelible character of a child of God; the frowns of Heaven are superseded by its smiles, and an invitation to eternal bliss is inscribed upon the soul's hopeful banner. What but the death of the Man-God could effect such a change? From His death and from it only the material water of Baptism has received the miraculous quality which enables it to wash even immaterial, immortal spirits, men's souls, and the words of that Sacrament have drawn their life and the power to sanctify. Thus by virtue of the death of Christ, each Christian has been "born again of water and the Holy Ghost." His death has thrown open, in this Sacrament, the portals of life to as many as wish to enter, and once they have crossed the threshold He numbers them among the living members of His mystical body, the Church, wherein await them the means by which the millions, during the ages of her existence, have become Saints, and attained their immortal crowns above. From children of darkness they have been transformed into children of light—" Called out of darkness into the admirable light of Christ." Alas! that so many know not this light; that so many, through their own fault, live and die in the original darkness in which they were enveloped on entering the world! Great God! how gloomy the outlook is for the millions of the future, since so-called teachers of Christianity have concluded to treat this as they have dealt with the other Sacraments instituted for man's sanctification and salvation by your divine Son! That is to say: deny its necessity and effects, notwithstanding the clear, the unmistakable teaching of our blessed Redeemer. Oh how many, owing to this terrible perversion and nullification of the most sacred tenets of Christianity, we daily meet, who call themselves Christians, and, God pity them! they are not more so than the poor Chinaman who, contrary to the divine whisperings of an interior voice, persists in his dismal superstition! Words could not be more explicit than those of Our Lord showing the necessity of this Sacrament. Who could understand His words to Nicodemus in any other sense than that given them by His Church, His very mouthpiece: "Verily, verily, I say to thee, except a man be born again of water and the Holy Ghost, he cannot enter into the kingdom of God"? What a strange perversion of the sense of the text it would be to say that Our Lord did not teach the necessity of Baptism, when he said to the Apostles, as He commissioned them to preach the Gospel to all nations: "He that believeth and is baptized shall be saved." But to pursue arguments of this nature should be neither necessary nor profitable so far as you are concerned.

All the blessings that have come to us, and they are legion, by "the laver of regeneration and renovation of the Holy Ghost" have been bestowed upon us because of our covenant with God on the solemn occasion of our Baptism. We have been raised to the rank of children of God; we have been surrounded with the spiritual plenty of God's kingdom on earth, and we have been made heirs to the everlasting joys of His eternal kingdom above. But, as in His dealings with man, God never encroaches upon that freedom of will by which He has made man the masterpiece of His creation on earth, He has exacted that the unconstrained acceptance of these glorious advantages and prerogatives be sealed by the strongest and most solemn engagement which man can enter into with his God. By the terms of this covenant we have been held to articles of agreement, which have demanded fulfilment, under the penalty of forfeiture, of the rights and privileges set forth. Must it not seem clear to some, if they will but give the matter thought, that they have been very far from living up to their solemn engagement? True, they have retained the faith, but a lifeless faith, such as those have that deny God and the faith which He has given them, by their works. A man's professions are to little purpose when his actions are wanting in conformity. The world is fairly sick, aye, lamentably sick with people " who make profession of knowing God, but deny Him in their works." A Catholic of this type is the most inconsistent being on earth, and where is the parish without members that have but a barren, lifeless faith, and nothing more? Have we not our number of such people in this parish? Are there not, in this Catholic community, persons whose indifference in the practise of their religion is an open book which all can read? Is it not clear to us that their lives are not those that would warrant that they have complied with the conditions of their solemn engagement with their God? And if they have not, what has been the consequence? They have been guilty of high treason in renouncing their solemn allegiance to their King and their God; they have violated the conditions on the observance of which depended their enjoyment of the glorious privileges and prerogatives awarded them in Baptism. And for what have they thus basely abandoned their God and forfeited all the blessings with which He rewards fidelity? Go ask their passions. Avarice will claim its share; sensual pleasures will sing out for theirs; so that for a living, which they would have in any case, or for the gratification of beastly appetites, they have sold their birthrights. See, O man! if one be here whose life has been a direct contradiction to his baptismal covenant, what you have done. How long will it be thus with you? Are you not yet tired of abusing the mercy of the good God? Remember that this may be the last merciful warning that He will extend to you. Say once for all that you will no longer abuse the mercy of your loving Saviour, who bled and died to procure the graces conferred on you in Baptism.

Let all of us raise our minds and our hearts to-day in grateful thanks to God for the great Sacrament of Baptism, and the spiritual riches which flowed into our souls as the saving waters came down upon our heads; let us deplore, from the depths of our souls, that we have not been more faithful to those graces, and more unflinching in the allegiance which we solemnly vowed to our God at the hallowed font.

XXXII.

SEVENTH SUNDAY AFTER PENTECOST.

"For the wages of sin is death; but the grace of God, life everlasting in Jesus Christ our Lord."—Rom. vi. 23.

After St. Paul's powerful exhortation to the Romans urging them to cease to serve their passions and give themselves with hearty good will to God's service, he cited the important motive which our mother, the Church, fails not to keep before the minds of her children. He reminded them that the slaves of sin hasten to everlasting death, but that a life of grace is sure to terminate in endless bliss. To-day in his epistle he reminds us of the same grave truth, which it becomes us to weigh more seriously than many have done in the past. No man in the full possession of his reason can ponder seriously the words of the Apostle without terror, if he be in mortal sin, or without earnestly renewing a resolution to persevere, if he be in a state of grace. The great mischief is that by far the greater number of the congregation in whose hearing they are announced, bring not home to themselves their awful meaning as their own individual concern. This accounts for their continuance in the commission of serious sins, and their persistence in stolid indifference concerning matters of the soul. The truths of God which they hear, but heed not, are intended to give them the alarm of the risk they run by living in sin, and to arouse them to a sense of their duty to their souls, but they fall short of their effect, for they seldom reach the heart. Do sensible people generally receive the admonitions of their family physicians so lightly? Indeed not, and those who do fail in promptness in complying with their orders are considered reckless and peculiar. Were this recklessness more common, sickness would be more prevalent and deaths more frequent. The rampancy of sin and the frequency of miserable deaths are due in a great measure to the little heed paid to what God's representatives utter regarding the evil and everlasting misery of sin, and the blessing and everlasting happiness of grace. Knowing as he must that he has no warrant for one hour of his life, that it entirely rests with God when and where to snap the thread of his life, could any man of sense listen to the words of St. Paul: "The wages of sin is death, but that of grace life everlasting," bring their meaning home as addressed to himself, and continue the slave of sin and stranger of a life of grace? What then but a lack of serious thought is accountable for the sins and religious indifference among Christians? Oh, that men would think half as much of providing for their souls in eternity as they do concerning the maintenance of their bodies for the few short years of this life! What a change would be wrought upon the face of the earth! How much more acceptable to Heaven would be the ways of men on earth!

Who are they who are hastening to the dire wages of sin, and who are they who are on their way to everlasting happiness? The unthinking millions that never ask themselves in the light of God's truth why they are here and whither they must go, like the unfortunate one on his way to death, the penalty of his misdeeds at the hands of human justice, are on their way to eternal death, at the hands of divine justice. With what vehemence they condemn the malice, the deeds, and the reckless thoughtlessness of the man who has fallen into the hands of human justice, whilst they have God's word for it that their malice, deeds, and reckless thoughtlessness are about to cast them into the hands of divine justice, where awaits them eternal punishment! See, O man of sinful malice, of wicked deeds, of deplorable thoughtlessness concerning the truths of God, what is before you! That man who goes to the scaffold erected for the vindication of human justice, whose fate you deem the most deplorable that can befall a human being, has ample time to prepare and fortify himself against that infinitely more deplorable fate to which you are being hurried by your spiritual enemies, and which your present manner of living strongly foreshadows you will reach. Why all these gloomy associations of thought and sentiment for another, and none for yourself, whose fate is likely to be so much worse? It is true you have it in your power to escape the terrible fate awaiting you, whilst that poor man has it not; but you should not forget that, like the power to live, it is not at your disposition as long as you will, and that there are degrees in the justice of God beyond which His mercy will not be abused. The degree beyond which you will not be allowed to abuse divine mercy is as great a mystery to you as the time of your death. When the abuse of divine mercy will have reached its limit for you, the time will have come when the words of God will be applicable to your case:

"Then shall they call upon Me and I will not hear," etc. From this it should seem necessary to say that the comparatively small number of the world's inhabitants earnestly in quest of eternal happiness is made up of those who allow not the world and its distractions to interfere with their serious thoughtfulness of God's truth. You here before me are so many open books to the all-seeing eye of God; He knows every shadow of the lamentable state of those who are in deadly sin; He knows you, who are deeply religious; and He knows those who are superficially so. We have some knowledge of each other, but His knowledge of man is complete. Supposing then that God would have an angel descend into our midst; who would they be whom God's angelic servant would single out as the most pleasing to Him, as the most deeply religious, as those earnestly in quest of the reward of a life of grace? Emphatically the members of the congregation "who hear His word and keep it" in their hearts by serious thought, to be produced in its fruit in their daily lives. The man who thinks seriously on the truths of God will be humble; he will know his absolute dependence on God; he will be a man of heartfelt prayer, and these suffice to make him a truly good man. Who will argue that an extensive education is required to have a mind disciplined for serious thought on even eternal truths? Were those of Our Lord's disciples who profited most from His divine utterances the enjoyers of very extensive educations? Who were they? Twelve poor fishermen, farmers, laborers, mechanics, and traders in merchandise. These brought home to themselves the divine doctrines of Our Lord; they thought upon them and extracted from them humility, their knowledge of man's absolute dependence on God, and the necessity of holy prayer. Precisely the same divine truths have we for consideration, and in proportion as we allow them to sink into our hearts by slow, serious thought, will we be religious. It should not be forgotten that there is one within who presents to those whose hearts are disposed, the truths uttered by the priest, the external teacher, so clearly and convincingly that the dullest and most illiterate are put in possession of subtle religious conceptions, which the most learned would fail to extract from books. How often have the most learned men been surprised to hear the most profound religious utterances from illiterate, but thoughtful and deeply religious persons! A good disposition of heart, and the truths explained by the priest afford the occasion in which the Holy Ghost can teach more to the purpose in an instant than could be extracted from books in a lifetime. Thus we see why the awful truths of our text are so often heard without fruit. Shall their annunciation to-day prove useless to the people of this congregation? If, as they have often done before, the members of the congregation will forget as soon as they have left the church, that " the wages of sin is death eternal, and that of grace everlasting bliss," yes, but if on the contrary these words will be pondered at leisure, they will bear excellent fruit.

XXXIII.

EIGHTH SUNDAY AFTER PENTECOST.

" But if by the spirit you mortify the deeds of the flesh, you shall live."—Rom. viii. 13.

After St. Paul had forcibly reminded the Romans of the woful consequence of living in slavish servitude to the sinful appetites of the flesh, by way of contrast he reminded them by the word "live" of the untold bliss which God has in store for those who, in the interest of their souls, refuse to feed their greedy passions. The distinctive difference between the sinner and the saint is that the former, led by the animal instincts of his inferior nature, gives pre-eminence to the flesh, but the latter, led by the aspirations of his soul, aided by divine grace, grants it to the spirit. This is in perfect harmony with the design of the Creator, that is in direct contradiction to His intent, and the forerunner of that eternal ruin which the enemy of God and man desires for every member of the human family. The flesh then must be the servant within the power of the spirit to discipline when and where it may be needed. Thus man will be as his Creator intended —a man, not a human brute. This position, in the face of the enemies that labor constantly to drag him down, man can never hold without divine grace. As an infant to three giants is he to the devil, the world, and the flesh, without divine aid; but God with him, the soul will be queen of his nature, and the body the servant which she will command and make obey, no matter how much devils may rage and the world tempt. To succeed, therefore, in mortifying the deeds of the flesh by the spirit, we must make sure, and lay in a good stock of divine grace, by the perpetual and proper use of the God-given means. Need you be reminded of their nature and their whereabouts? Ah, no; you the children of the Church are within God's treasury on earth, and therefore the means of spiritual riches are on all sides of you. We will, however, confine our thoughts to a few.

Every Christian is before high Heaven pledged in the most solemn manner to show that he values his soul more than his body. To be true to this engagement, as we have considered, he must have aid from above. Now the means of procuring the divine assistance, which is always at our disposal, irrespective of condition or circumstances, and which God is most desirous that we should everywhere and at all times use, is prayer. We have His divine word for it that His aid will not be wanting to us if we pray. No one is excepted in this divine promise; the sinner, thanks to the infinite mercy of the good God, as well as the saint will be heard if he go in good earnest in holy prayer to the throne of mercy. Suffice it to say that this condition on which God promises all we need, is the very least He could exact of us, whilst at the same time it is the most important, since no other condition can be duly and acceptably complied with unless preceded, accompanied, and followed by this. Truly Christian people begin, continue, and end eveything by prayer, and whatever cannot be thus sanctified they conscientiously shrink from as not becoming them to do. Hence, were I to say to you: "Mortify by the spirit the deeds of the flesh," before you had learned to go to the throne of divine mercy in holy prayer, as you must see, I would speak to little purpose. St. Paul, when he wrote these words, supposed that those for whom he intended them had acquired the habit of prayer. Prayer must most assuredly precede mortification; hence the admonition to pray must necessarily go before that to mortify. In fact, prayer itself is one of the most valuable, fruitful, and to God acceptable, species of mortification. The Sacraments are so many fountains of divine grace, and of two of them must the Christian who wishes to obey the admonition of the Apostle frequently every year receive grace—Penance and the most holy Eucharist. We might call the worthy reception of these sacraments prayer in its perfection. He who prays aright will often, during the year, enter the confessional and appear at the Communion railing, and he who thus frequently appears will pray aright. By frequently refortifying the soul with the graces which never fail to come to her from the worthy reception of those Sacraments, that Christian vigor so necessary in order to preserve the authority of the spirit over the flesh is maintained. No Christian can be ignorant of this. Whoever will look back upon his past life will detect that the months during which his prayers were seldom, or only very indifferently said, marked the intervals in which these Sacraments were not received, and as a sad consequence the spirit was at the mercy of the flesh. On the other hand, when fidelity to these sacred duties was the rule, the spirit had control. Just so is it with you to-day. If fervent prayer mark your days; if the frequent reception of the Sacraments be your wont, your spirit is in control. These are the sure signs by which you can pass upon yourself. Another admirable means of procuring divine grace is to assist at all the Masses that our circumstances in life will possibly admit. Of course all are aware that it is no matter of option, but a strict obligation to hear Mass on Sundays and Holy days, but besides this, all who can and are desirous to keep their souls well fortified with divine succor, should do so on other days. The time of Mass is the time by excellence in which to go with our petitions to the throne of grace. God is then being honored and pleased by the great sacrifice, infinite in value, and the richest and most valuable graces can be obtained by devout worshippers. After direct devotion to God there is no devotion so calculated to elicit divine succor as that to the most blessed Mother of Our Lord—she is called in the litany "Mother of divine grace." It is a well sustained fact that those who are really devout to her are sufficiently strong of spirit to keep the flesh in healthy Christian subjection. Show me one that is truly devout to the Mother of God, and I will show you a person who "by the spirit mortifies the deeds of the flesh." Mark what I say; it is a matter of the very greatest importance to have regular set devotions, which you will satisfy at stated times, arranged according to the circumstances of your lives. Once you acquire a habit of this, then you can consider you have made some real progress. A fit and start devotion is very far from what you need to sustain the spirit in control over the flesh. Were you to thus minister food to your body, it would ere long be unable to cope with its duties for want of strength. So it is with the spirit;

it wants its regular daily sustentance, and if deprived of that, strength begins to wane, and the flesh soon gets control. Oh, the large number of Christians who thus crush the spirit within them and simply lead animal lives! Their lives are a frustration of the designs of God, and a direct contradiction to their rational constitution. The spirit should rule, for so God designed, and to crush the spirit by giving the flesh the supremacy is to live like the soulless animal of the field, a prey to animal appetites, likes, and dislikes.

You see then, dear people, that to live as men, and not as animals, we must "By the spirit mortify the deeds of the flesh," and you must also see from what has been said that it is impossible to do this violence to the flesh without aid from God. All those who resolve to have the spiritual part of their nature, true to the designs of the Creator, in control, must not fail to make constant use of the means by which grace will be assured to their souls. Pray, confess, communicate, after the manner of all good Catholics.

XXXIV.

NINTH SUNDAY AFTER PENTECOST.

"Wherefore he that thinketh himself to stand, let him take heed lest he fall."—1. Cor. x. 12.

When we hear people putting the worst construction on the mistakes and short-comings of their neighbor, we can be convinced that they have not yet learned to know themselves, nor acquired a very deep knowledge of the weakness of poor human nature. One would imagine to hear them talk, that for them to commit themselves in a like way would be as impossible as for truth to become error. But the Apostle did not think as they do, and his knowledge of human nature, it is to be hoped, they will hesitate to call in question. The man of genuine Christian sense knows himself, at least, well enough to conceive the possibility, if not perhaps in similar circumstances the probability, of such weaknesses as he detects in others, been portrayed in himself. Hence instead of making the worst of his neighbor's faults he deplores them, does what he can to correct him of them, trembles for himself, and for his future guidance learns a fresh lesson. Passing strange, but all the same true, is it that those who are weak themselves are remarkable for their want of mercy towards their weak neighbor, whilst their distinctive difference is not greater than that circumstances serve to conceal the weaknesses of the one, whilst they expose those of the other. Hypocrisy of course is the motive of such people, and for them our subject admits of no more than an incidental remark. No man who has the remotest knowledge of himself, though he were as free from faults as is possible for man to be, but must feel how aptly the sentiments of the Apostle apply to him. He will be far from imagining that because he now stands, that therefore to fall is not even among the possibilities for him. Far will be from him the practice, alas! too common, and generally the forerunner of a fall, of assuming to himself any uncharitable license to talk at will concerning the short-comings and mistakes of others. On the contrary, his aim it will always be, save when duty demands a different manner of action, to let the thought of them die within him. But whilst from a motive of charity to others he thus behaves, from a like motive to himself, his memory fails not to faithfully retain for his better guidance a recollection of the circumstances which proved the occasion of his neighbor's mistakes. Though, he will say to himself, I am free from those faults which I and others perceive in him, were I to trust myself to associates such as his, or were I to resort to those places to which he seems to have not unfrequent recourse, or were I to allow myself to be so engrossed with matters temporal, and give little or no attention to the practice of my religion, could I expect better than to be guilty of the same mistakes? Ah, no; for I am warned by Truth Itself that, if I love the danger and follow my sentiments in its regard, the consequence will be a grace-wrecked soul in time, and if I fly not from it before God's justice takes the place of His mercy, a damned soul for eternity. "He that loves the danger will perish therein." Nor will my own experience allow me to doubt that I rob myself of all source of strength when I give up the practice of my religion, or use it occasionally only for the sake of appearance, without any motive of acquiring strength. It would indeed, will the sensible man who stands say, be a miracle were I to deprive myself of my only source of strength, the practice of my religion, and expose myself to the dangers of sin, and after all, save the two sins already committed, not betray some of the weaknesses and mistakes which I now so much deplore in others. The man who will thus always reason is one who, as the Apostle tells him, takes heed, and for him there is little danger of a fall. But let him who sets little value on the strength acquired from the practice of religion, and who so swells with presumption as to imagine that associates, places, or all other circumstances could not prevail on him to be as weak or foolish as his neighbor, remember that he is preparing the way to have, if not men, because of his wordly cunning, at least devils point the finger of scorn at him. How they gloat over the thousands now in eternity whom he faithfully imitates! The Apostle spoke not in vain. It is a small matter to be laughed at by men, compared with that of being laughed at and ridiculed by devils. Oh, the number of Catholics that are complete laughing-stocks for devils, and seem inclined to be so throughout eternity, though before men they command respect as ordinarily good people! A lacking in the practice of religion rarely counts for much in the motley communities of to-day, but with God and the enemy of souls it is quite otherwise. The criterion from which a true conclusion can be reached as to whether a man stands with God, or has fallen a prey of the evil one, is the practice of his religion. If it be such as pleases God, but displeases His enemy, all is well; the man stands; if it displeases God, but pleases the enemy, then no matter how the man stands in the estimation of men, he is a fallen man. Alas! how many such there are in every parish; we have our share of them in ours. Let those who stand take warning and ever remember that what has happened to the indifferent of our parish who have thus fallen, will occur to the very best of those who stand, should they try to live without practical religion. The world is cursed with drunkards, thieves, high and low, lecherous wretches, and unprincipled people of every grade, because practical religion is not known to a large majority of its inhabitants. We hear the cry of reform here, and the cry of new departures for good there, but no genuine reform is beheld where practical religion is not even known. Their mistake is in deeming real reform to be within the unaided power of man; whilst no such reform is possible without aid from above, and practical religion, so little in use, is the means by which divine aid is obtained. People who try to make drunkards sober men by force, are engaged in a fruitless work, and the same may be said of the work of those who labor by any other way than leading people to practical religion, to correct the vices that are to be deplored in every community. Till the law-makers, till the law-executors have learned to have more respect for religion, there is but little hope that notorious law-breakers will be much improved. And so long as education, such as is given, and the example of men whose stations demand better things of them, tend to lessen regard for practical religion, the hope of a transition from vice to virtue, save among those who are led to reform by teachers whose lives conform to their teaching, has no foundation. It is clear then, that in proportion as individuals or communities are practically religious, will virtue or vice prevail.

It seems to me that we have ample matter in what has been considered to deduce conclusions, each in his own case, that will not be without fruit if followed. It is not all at once that people sink into that indifference to the practice of their religion, which is at the bottom of those vices which they deplore in others. Every one who desires to hearken to the sentiments of the Apostle, as expressed in our text, should, whilst charitably silent regarding the short-comings of others, learn the lesson which they teach, and examine himself on his religion, especially his feeling of dependance on God, his daily prayers, his reception of the Sacraments, and though last, not least, his inclination to seek God's aid in time of trial, and his disposition to tender thanks to Him in time of success. The truly wise will only be satisfied when they find themselves advancing in these hallowed practices, for to grow cool would bespeak an approaching fall. They know they stand, therefore they "take heed least they fall."

XXXV.

TENTH SUNDAY AFTER PENTECOST.

"And no man can say, the Lord Jesus, but by the Holy Ghost."
—1. Cor. xii. 3.

It shall seem to all who really set value on serving God and saving their souls, how vastly important it is according to the words of the Apostle, to be under the divine influence of the Holy Ghost. Nothing can be clearer, as expressed in the words of our text, than man's inability without the Holy Ghost. Absolutely nothing can he do when his soul is not the habitation of that divine Spirit. How very few really give the heartfelt thought to this most serious matter which it deserves! This thoughtlessness of Christians accounts for the large number of lives that are so many blanks before God, as regards supernatural merit. A man without the Holy Ghost cannot merit, for He who should be the motive and end of his every work is forgotten. Worse still when the Spirit of God is not within, the spirit of evil fills His place. Under the divine influence of the Holy Ghost it is quite possible for a man to attain the highest degree of virtue, as is clear from the lives of those who have been, by the lustre of their virtues, the glory of the Church in every age. All one has to do in whose soul the Holy Ghost abides is to co-operate with His divine grace accompanied suggestions, and the days of his life will be filled with works of merit. He even holds out to all blessed by His divine presence the grace to co-operate, so that whoever fails, does so culpably. Under the vigilant and fostering care of our mother the Church throughout the world, people walk the earth whose souls are the habitation of the divine Spirit, though but the comparative few distinguish themselves by the lustre of their virtues. Whilst very often persons are at fault in their lack of co-operation for not reaching a higher degree of virtue, it is likewise true that, though the Holy Ghost amply provides all in whose souls He abides with the graces to be virtuous, there are those to whom, for His own wise ends, the gifts of His bounty are attended more profusely. Like the gifts of nature, the gifts of the supernatural order are divided according to the good pleasure of God, and not without reasons worthy of His divine wisdom. The one great work which He has in view for all—the one for which He created and redeemed us—is foremost; and when He has attended to each sufficient grace to attain this, He distributes His other supernatural favors according to the designs which He has in view for each individual. As for instance, the Blessed Virgin stands pre-eminent as the most favored child of God, positively and negatively so, because of the sublime station which He had allotted to her in His eternal counsels. The mother of His divine Son required the highest gifts of grace possible for a human creature, and complete freedom from aught of evil, original and actual. Therefore through a most wonderous miracle He fully qualifies her for the most exalted station that could be assigned to a creature by the most sublime prerogatives which He sealed with a confirming grace. In like manner, according to the stations in life which

He intends them to fill, does God qualify by His gifts and graces all His other servants. All have their allotted destinies in this world, the requirements which demand special, natural, and supernatural qualifications for the worthy discharge of their respective duties. The importance of the exact fulfilment of the responsibilities of this vocation will appear when we consider that the common destiny in the life to come is, to say the least, in great danger when this of the present is treated with indifference or neglect. Hence, whilst the Holy Ghost furnishes graces sufficient to all to virtuously discharge their respective duties and comply with the obligations with their states in life, as is clear, His bounty is diverse according to the demands of each one's vocation. That all will receive sufficient from Him to become saints, if they will, is evident from the fact that every vocation is represented by saints in heaven. Every soul that has passed the portals of heaven has done so by the power of the Holy Ghost, for as the Apostle tells us, without Him we cannot say the Lord Jesus with supernatural merit, much less can we lead lives acceptable to God and worthy of heaven.

When, therefore, we behold people most faithful in the discharge of all their Christian duties; when we behold them prompt and devoted in their attendance at the holy Mass on Sundays and days of obligation; when we behold them frequently approaching holy Communion; and when we see and hear them exercise charity, even in the most trying circumstances towards their enemies as well as their friends, we can be sure that all this is the outcome of the grace of the Holy Ghost and their own faithful co-operation therewith. In the wise judgment of the man enlightened by the Holy Ghost and co-operating with His grace, the creature's most devoted service, whilst it is all that he can give, is but a meagre return for the inestimable gifts of God's goodness, even though the attaining of heaven were not in question. The man thus enlightened values objects and works not after the fashion of those, whatever may be their gifts of education, to whom the Holy Ghost is not welcome, but in direct harmony with the example of the saints before whose wisdom that of the world is the height of folly. He knows that there is One to whom he owes his existence, to whom he is responsible, and to whom he will have to render a strict account when life's journey will be over; and in proportion as objects and works serve to make him, according to His good pleasure are they valuable in his sight. Sin, therefore, he utterly hates in all its varied phases, as the great insult to God's majesty; and the one great evil which can destroy his supernatural life and his brilliant prospects for eternity; whatever directly or indirectly tends to enable him to comply with the demands of God, he loves; and the circumstances of the last trial at the tribunal of the Judge to whom he is responsible for his every thought, word, and action, are not unfrequently before his mind. All this too, is the happy result of the blight and grace of the Holy Ghost in conjunction with his own co-operation—" When He will come, He will convince the world of sin, of justice, and of judgment."

How sad it is that so many make light of sin, seldom or never feel their responsibilities to God, and give little heed to what their faith teaches them regarding their last end! These are clear signs that the

Holy Ghost is not within; that, alas! the spirit that has in view their eternal ruin, holds sway. Of such unhappy people, and they unfortunately are numerous, the contrary of what we said of those in whose souls abide the Spirit of God, may be advanced. Their case is very deplorable. Sound their motives through life; oh, how unworthy they are of Christians! Their lives are a hollow deception without merit! Could they have peace with that spirit, the wicked author of all man's unhappiness within their souls? Who are they? All those who are in a state of mortal sin. By this they have driven the Holy Ghost from their souls, and invited and welcomed the devil to take up his abode with them. As persons in whose souls the Spirit of God abides are capable of attaining the very highest degree of virtue possible for a Christian, so those in whose unfortunate souls the friend of evil abides are capable of descending to the commission of the most degrading vices. The pleasure of the evil one within is to degrade the Christian as much as possible by plunging him into the very lowest depths of vice. Alas! how often has he the satisfaction of succeeding in this! Is there one here under his accursed sway? Let the conscience of each speak. Is there one here in mortal sin? If so, then the devil has one unfortunate dupe in our midst. Oh is it not well if he has but one? is it not well if but one of this congregation is without the Holy Ghost, and therefore helpless in doing aught worthy of supernatural merit? Let me ask that one who is the better off: he or the man beside him in whose soul the Holy Ghost abides, and hence whose every prayer and work finds favor with God?

XXXVI.

ELEVENTH SUNDAY AFTER PENTECOST.

"For I am the least of the Apostles, who am not worthy to be called an Apostle, because I persecuted the Church of God."—1. Cor. xv. 9.

All without exception can find in these words of the Apostle a lesson of great value to themselves. What true humility they bespeak? When he called himself "the least of the Apostles" he uttered the honest sentiments of his heart; when he proclaimed himself "unworthy to be called an Apostle" it was not a latent pride, but true humility which prompted the expression; and when, as a reason for his unworthiness he urged his work against the Church before his conversion, he showed that by the constant recollection of the evils of his past life, he conquered pride and put himself in possession of true, unfeigned humility. Is not this great model well worthy of our imitation? How few there are who cannot, if they will, look back on their past lives and read on their pages what unworthy creatures they are! Oh, the humiliating picture the lives of some will present! All doubtless will find sufficient in their past years to make them feel, when considered in a true Christian spirit, how little before God and man they really are. It is the way of those who are truly humble never for any considerable time to lose sight of the humiliating scenes in their past lives, and especially do they keep a vivid recollection of them when existing circumstances in their behalf might prove conducive to pride. In this they follow the hallowed example of the millions who have possessed real virtue and done honor to the Christian name, one of the most brilliant of whom was St. Paul himself. In the life of every one there are past circumstances known to himself, the memory of which serve better than that of others to make him better in his own eyes, hence the frequent recollection of them will prove of untold value to him in the cultivation of that most necessary virtue, true Christian humility. Thus past sins repented of can be made the occasions of acquiring great and necessary virtues. The absolute necessity of humility should not be lost sight of unless we mean that our Christianity shall be nothing more than a passing, idle pretence. To prove the necessity of this virtue, it should suffice to quote the words of sacred writ: "God rejects the proud, and gives His grace to the humble." If with candor of purpose any one here will examine carefully the varied vicissitudes of his life, the stages during which he has been thoughtless, indifferent, and without taste for things spiritual, and the periods during which, on the contrary, he has led a good Christian life, if indeed he can call to mind such happy seasons, he will find that the pride of self-sufficiency marked his ways in the dark stages of sin, and that an humble dependance on God has been the real secret of his happy periods. Happy, I say, because only the humble know what true happiness, as far as it can be enjoyed in this life, is. The proud man is a prey to thousands of disquieting occasions from which the man of humility is saved. God demands of every man, whether he be a king on the throne or a laborer in the ditch, a "contrite and humble heart," and where this is wanting there is no true virtue. No one can fail to see how reasonable this demand is. Are all not sinners? Should a man assert the contrary, he is branded by St. John as a liar. Can we therefore be received into favor till we are contrite? and how can we be contrite without being at the same time humble? Hence you must see, the difference between those who are true penitents and the unfortunate Christians that only pretend to repent, is that the former are humble and the latter are devoid of that virtue. And no one need be informed that a true, not a mock repentance is acceptable to God. What then, O man of pride! will justify your conduct? Is it not as clear as day that you must either part with your pride, or during your whole life long abuse the most sacred means which God has given for the sanctification and salvation of man? Though absolutely necessary for our sanctification and salvation, and therefore of the most unquestionable value to us, large indeed is the number of Christians who make daily journey towards eternity without it, because for want of due consideration they fail to recognize its value. So wanting is the knowledge of some in respect to this virtue, they imagine the practise of it demands of them to act in a rather foolish role. It is hardly necessary to say it is not the Spirit of God who prompts them to entertain such notions. Surely no Christian will imagine it savors of foolishness, according to God, to imitate our blessed Lord, His Virgin Mother, and His saints. According to the world it may seem so. The more humble we become the more truly do we imitate them. Humility has been the foundation of all the greatness of the true and most distinguished followers of Our Lord. When life's journey for them was over, their greatness was valued at His judgment-seat according to their humility. Thus too shall our lives be passed upon before reward or punishment shall be assigned us. Should it not seem then, that it is impossible for us to overestimate the value of this virtue? The more the esteem of it grows in us, the more earnestly will we exert ourselves to attain its highest degrees. Our hearts will ardently long to advance in it, and fervent prayers will daily ascend from us for divine assistance to attain the object of our longings. Daily occasions will not be wanting to us for its exercise, and they will be embraced profitably in proportion to our previous prayerful preparation. Since without God we can do nothing, all that it is possible for us to do must of necessity be done through His assistance, obtained chiefly by daily, fervent prayer. How edifying it is to see persons virtuously submissive to the will of God in all, even the most trying, circumstances! how it makes us reflect upon our want of virtue to behold worthy persons conceal, as far as possible, whatever could command for them the esteem or applause of men; to see them betray a species of mortification when their worthy deeds, notwithstanding their vigilance to prevent it, should have reached the public and drawn forth what they most feared, the applause of men! Thanks to the Church, the mother of saints, the world is hallowed every day with the lives of such people. Yes, they not only fly from the world's gaze to do their noble work, but they bear in meekness and patience its ridicules, reproaches, and affronts. The spirit with which the Apostles edified all future generations when they "rejoiced at being accounted worthy to suffer in the cause of their divine Master," is daily being exercised throughout the world by the most saintly characters, without noise or trumpet. Now, all this is the result of the divine assistance elicited by prayers sent up from hearts ardently desirous of the highest degrees of humility. What is true in respect to all other gifts from above, is certainly so of that most necessary virtue—humility; ask it and you will be made its happy possessor.

From all this it should seem to us that in order to imitate the virtue taught us in the words of our text, we must first, by serious thought on its absolute necessity, learn to esteem it; then we should petition divine aid to acquire it, by a penitential recollection of our past defects, and a truly Christian appreciation of all the occasions of exercising it which daily present themselves. No one can doubt of success who will thus proceed in quest of this sterling virtue on which our comfort both here and in the life to come so absolutely depends. Let, then, our prayer for a deeper Christian humility daily go up to the throne of God. Let us never forget that heaven is the reward of humility, and hell the punishment of pride.

XXXVII.
TWELFTH SUNDAY AFTER PENTECOST.

"For if the ministration of condemnation be glory, much more the ministration of justice aboundeth in glory."—2. Cor. iii. 9.

The Apostle, in this epistle, taught the Corinthians the esteem and respect they should have for God's ministers. He leads them to understand that they should not consider them as mere men, but as "fit ministers of God," qualified by His Spirit to represent Him in continuing the work begun by His divine Son. He introduced a comparison between the ministration of Moses and that of the priests of the New Law, showing the infinite superiority of the latter. From this he made it clear to them that, since God exacted from the people in the Old Law, esteem and respect for His representatives so vastly inferior to those of His priesthood of the New Law, with greater reason does He demand these expressions of regard and veneration for His ministers of the New Dispensation. It will not indeed be unprofitable for us to give our thoughts to-day to the great dignity of the priesthood, since the words directed by the Apostle to the Corinthians were intended to instruct all Christians.

Our blessed Lord began the great work of Christianizing, civilizing, sanctifying, and saving the world, and when the time of His mortal career was about spent, He called, ordained, and commissioned His Apostles to continue the stupendous work, investing them with power to call, ordain, and commission others, who in like manner would continue the work, and provide for its continuance when their time should be spent. Every priest, therefore, has been called, ordained, and, when sent by his superiors, commissioned to do the word which our blessed Lord began. He is the duly authorized representative of Jesus Christ, doing the very work that He Himself would be doing had it pleased Him to remain, instead of only three and thirty, nineteen hundred years as the man-God among men. The priest, therefore, is a man filling a divine destiny, which entered in connection with him into the eternal councils of God, who from all eternity called him, and in time of ordination stamped his soul with the divine character of his eternal priesthood,—the priesthood of Jesus Christ. He is even more than a mere representative of Christ, for every good Christian is that; he is in a certain sense a second Christ, because he is invested with power which only Christ and His priest can exercise. Even official representation is suggestive of limitation of power, but no such limitation has been put upon the power with which Christ has invested His priests. The priest as such is no more limited than was Christ Himself,—it is God's own power given to the priesthood of the New Law. Was there a limit placed to the commissioned priest's power of forgiving sins when Christ said to him: "Whose sins you shall forgive they are forgiven; whose sins you shall retain they are retained"? Is this not the very same power which Christ exercised, and therefore caused His enemies to say that "none but God can forgive sins"? True, none but God can forgive sins; and when they uttered these words, Jesus Christ, who is God as well as man, was in the act of forgiving them, as He does when the priest, using God's power, pronounces the sacred and saving words of absolution. In the great tribunal of consciences where every one who has come to the use of reason, under the penalty of eternal reprobation, is obliged to appear as a witness, to testify to all his offences against the law of God and His Church, the priest is duly constituted by God, both judge and jury. He passes upon the various cases as God Himself, and his work is ratified in the supreme court of heaven. Honored, esteemed, and respected should be the man so sublimely exalted by God; and eternally praised should God be for "having given such power to man," are the promptings of right reason and religion.

Not alone in his power to adjust the accounts between immortal souls and God does the great, the exalted, the sublime dignity of the priestly minister of Jesus Christ appear, but also in his God-given power over matter, and in his mission to God's people. The power of changing one ordinary substance into another, as that of water into wine, should suffice to single a man out, were he thus impowered, as one sublimely favored and exalted by God; but who can give serious thought without having the greatest respect for the person, to the power exercised by him, who changes two humble substances into that whose creation was the highest work of God,—the most sacred humanity of Jesus Christ. If the working of such a stupendous miracle by Our Lord Himself was pronounced by the great St. Thomas Aquinas "an abridgment of all the wonders He had ever wrought," what should be our estimate of the dignity of the man whom Christ has impowered to repeat this miracle every day of his priestly life! " Do this," said Christ to His priest in ordination, " in commemoration of Me." O sublime power, which raised the man thus invested, above all other creatures, above those who are by nature the masterpieces of God's creation—the angels! O wonderful condescension on the part of the great God, in investing a worm of the earth with His own divine power over consciences and substances!

Besides their God-given power, the ministers of Christ have a mission to teach the peoples of the world. The message which they bring is for the high and the low, the rich and the poor, the lettered and the unlettered, —in a word, for all the human beings to whom God has given existence, and for whom Christ shed His blood. The unwillingness of some to hear them, the propensity of others to raise up other teachers after their own fashion, and the indifference of those who believe but practise not what they believe, affect no more their divine authority to teach than the conduct of similar characters did that of Christ Himself. " As My Father hath sent Me, I also send you,"—" Go ye, therefore, and teach all nations—teaching them to observe all things whatsoever I have commanded you." Thus Our Lord proclaimed the mission of the ministers of His Church to the people of the world. It is stupid; it is a betrayal of deplorable ignorance of what all men should know, to deny their authority; and of all who are convinced of their authority to teach, but from motives of interest, or from an unreasonable prejudice, refuse to admit their convictions, we are constrained to say that a more desperate part it is impossible for them to act. Open, O man! God's sacred Book, and read what He has authorized to be penned there of His priestly-ministers! "For Christ therefore," says St. Paul, "we are ambassadors, God as it were exhorting by us. For Christ, we beseech you, be reconciled to God." "The lips of the priest shall keep knowledge, and they shall seek the law at his mouth, because he is the angel of the Lord of hosts." And again: "I preached the Gospel to you heretofore," says St. Paul, "and you received me as the angel of God, even as Christ Jesus." The absolute certainty of the divine mission of the ministers of Christ to teach the people of the whole world is the premises of the absolute certainty of the obligation of the people to hear and live according to their teaching. "He that hears you," says Our Lord to His ministers, "hears Me, and he that despises you despises Me."

Hence, it must seem clear to us that we owe, because of their divine vocation, the power of God which they exercise, and the message which they bring from God to us, great respect and regard for the person and character, and great fidelity to the teaching of the priestly-ministers of Christ.

XXXVIII.

THIRTEENTH SUNDAY AFTER PENTECOST.

"But the Scripture hath concluded all under sin, that the promise of the faith of Jesus Christ might be given to them that believe."—Galatians iii. 22.

Just as since the coming of Our Lord salvation has been impossible without faith in Him, so was it from the beginning. Only those were saved who had faith in Him and gave expression to their belief by their practice of the old God-given religion before His coming. From the moment in which God spoke His promise to the fallen parents of the human family, there has been but *one name* by virture of which man can reach the blissful end for which he has been created,— that name is Jesus. "There is no other name under heaven given to man whereby we must be saved, but the name Jesus only." Since on another occasion we gave our thoughts to the virtue of faith, and as it is to be hoped all of us are fully aware of the necessity of a lively, practical faith, it will doubtless be more to our profit to engage our minds to-day on the most hallowed name of Jesus. It signifies Saviour, for whom the God-fearing religious people of the Old Law so long sighed, and the God-loving, devoted people of the New Law have been, and shall ever be grateful. The infinitely blessed name Jesus then, is all things to us, for without it our existence would have been an eternal curse, because our sanctification, and by consequence our salvation would have been impossible: Since God promised a Redeemer there never has been a thought in the mind of man, there never has been a word uttered by human tongue, there never has been an action performed by rational being stamped with supernatural value other than that which has come from Jesus. All which was agreeable to heaven in the Old Law; all that has been pleasing to it in the New have been so by virture of the all holy name Jesus. Oh, then how dear to us this most precious name should be! How we should delight to pronounce it with all the respect of which we are capable! Is there one in eternity; is there one on the face of the earth to-day who with honesty of purpose and devotion of heart, in the name of Jesus, besought Heaven for any of these gifts which God has in store for man, and met with disappointment? Have we it not from the divine lips of Jesus Himself, in the most emphatic mode of His expression, that whatever we shall ask of the Father in His name shall be given to us? "Amen, amen, I say to you, if you ask the Father anything in My name He will give it you." Do we not believe the testimony of upright, conscientious men? In this text we have the testimony of God staking His divine veracity. Oh, the power of the sweet name Jesus! At the very sound of it on the tongue that does it honor, devils tremble, and the treasury of God's bounty flies open, and all desperate broodings vanish to give place to the most implicit confidence. Without this hope-inspiring name earth would be the ante-chamber of hell, and mankind would be in the throes of blank despair; heaven would never have among its citizens one of human kind, for the mercy refused to the rebellious angels would also have been denied to man. Only by this all-powerful name can men raise themselves up from earth to heaven, to be courtiers of God and associates of the angels in mansions the like of which "neither eye hath seen, ear heard, nor human heart conceived." Eternity alone should suffice, especially for the children of the Church of the New Law to do honor to this all-hallowed name.

Contrast to the mustard-seed the Church of nineteen centuries ago with the Church of to-day, which by virtue of the sacred name of Jesus, despite the powers of hell, despite the bloody persecutions of tyrants and anti-religious revolutions that have in one form or other assailed her, has grown to such wonderous proportions as to have within her fold people of every nation under heaven. Read the Acts of the Apostles. What striking grandeur presents itself when we read of the dead rushing back to life; the most malignant diseases which defied all human skill giving place to perfect health in the name of Jesus! Who can contemplate St. Paul calling back to life, in the name of Jesus, the young man who fell from the window, and St. Peter curing the man that had been lame from his birth, by saying: "Silver and gold I have none, but what I have I give thee; in the name Jesus of Nazareth, arise and walk," without experiencing a pleasing but awful thrill? But when we enter in thought those bloody amphitheatres of Rome; when we follow the cruel persecutions carried on in the most bloodthirsty manner, and call to mind that millions of martyrs in these dreadful circumstances down the ages have risen in the most glorious triumph over death, in all the terrible forms which devils could suggest, and wicked men could execute by virtue of the all-hallowed name of Jesus, we can realize what strength there is in store for all who will use this sacred name aright. Besides those grand champions of the faith who thus showed the virtue of the name of Jesus in their deaths, have we not millions of others who, though they have not been called upon to spill their blood professing the name Jesus, have not the less been martyrs, because by virtue of this sacred name they had died to themselves? Look up and behold those of every age who have conquered the world, the flesh and the devil by the name of Jesus,—" pillars in the eternal temple of God."

Oh that we could refrain from turning our thoughts to the terrible abuse of this all-hallowed name! Oh, how shocking it is to hear human tongue engaged in the profanation of the adorable name Jesus! How it almost freezes the blood of a true Christian's veins to hear the air ring, as is not unfrequently our sad wont, with the profanations of this holy name! But one of the worst circumstances of the horrid practice is the sad fact that Christians—Catholic's seem to vie with non-Christians in dishonoring this adorable name, to honor which their forefather's have bled and died in thousands. Great God, what disgraceful descendants of most worthy forefathers are to be found in the world to-day! In the language of angels and saints, which is that of Heaven, this adorable name is constantly honored; in the language of devils and the reprobate, which is that of hell, this hallowed name is continually profaned. Of which country is that language which those Christians speak, who from morning till night, at every turn, profane the holy name of Jesus ? Ah, dear people, it is needless to say it is not the language of Heaven, it must therefore be that of hell, and since that is their favorite mode of expression, it is easy to tell their country. Who would like to have his name abused as the sweet name of Jesus is abused by some Catholics? Is there a man here that would not resent the insult? Will Jesus allow His hallowed name to be thus abused with impunity? No, indeed, for sooner or later the divine vengeance will come upon those by whom it is thus abused. Oh, did time permit, what terrible examples could be advanced to show that Jesus will not permit His blessed name to be abused without making the guilty one in time, and perhaps throughout eternity, feel the weight of His justice!—" A man that sweareth much shall be filled with iniquity, and the scourge shall not depart from his house." Think well on that sentence, O ye who are addicted to the accursed habit of swearing by the adorable name of Jesus!

Since under heaven there is no other name by which we can escape hell, and reach heaven, besides the sweet name of Jesus, the profound respect, the all engrossing esteem, the supreme honor, which are its just claims from man, are evident. Have we always evinced this respect and esteem? have we always, when the occasion called for it, worshipped the name of Jesus from the very depths of our souls, as the all-hallowed name of the God made man, to whose love we are indebted for every thing of real value which we now possess, or which we hope to enjoy in the great future beyond the limits of this little world? What a blessing it would be if all who hear me could say, yes! Henceforth, whatever may have been the past, "we should look upon Jesus as the name of the Author and Finisher of our faith."

XXXIX.

FOURTEENTH SUNDAY AFTER PENTECOST.

"And they that are Christ's have crucified their flesh with the vices and concupiscences."—Gal. v. 24.

As we have directly considered on a former occasion the subject suggested by this text, we will now give our thoughts to two means, one positive and the other negative, which all utilize who succeed in practising the virtue therein inculcated. The first of these is good reading. The more one values the importance of feeding his mind with good, religious ideas, the more certainly will he appreciate Catholic books as a part of his household effects. The old saying in regard to companions may well be applied to books: "Show me the books you read, and I will tell you what manner of man you are." One of the most precious, because it is decidedly one of the most efficient means which we can make use of to stamp out all sensuality and enrich ourselves with the spirit of Our Lord, is reading such as has wrought these blessed effects in the millions whose lives in every age have shed lustre on our mother, the Church. Like them we must associate, by reading, their works with the learned and saintly men and women who have been bright ornaments in the Church in every age, but above all we should frequently put ourselves in the blessed company of Our Lord by careful readings of the sacred Gospels of our Bibles. Had we lived in the days of those learned and saintly men and women, they could not have favored us with more soul-moving sentiments than these which they have sent down the ages to us. We have in their works the beautiful indexes of their souls, teaching us to stamp out all sensuality and put on the spirit of Our Lord. Who can read the lives of the saints without being deeply impressed with the spirit of mortification with which those glorious champions of the cross are credited! Could there be more telling lessons of mortification than those we find in the Epistles of St. Paul? Oh, what untold good must come to the Christian soul that ponders devotedly the most admirable, sublime, and salutary utterance of our blessed Lord as contained in the Gospels! Impossible indeed is it to set too high a value on good reading. Who that has any experience of the blessed effects of good reading, will fail to acknowledge its great merit? The book is not afraid to speak on points and in circumstances which might combine to silence the human voice. It is no respecter of persons when the honor of God and good of souls are at stake. The rich as well as the poor; the learned as well as the unlettered; the influential as well as the least pretentious will have in it their duties explained, their sins condemned, their penalty deprived, and the most wholesome reproofs directed to them. What a valuable companion then a good, solid religious book is to any Christian! It is a remarkable fact that to find persons who have crushed out that antagonism so common even among Christians to mortification, and put on the spirit of Our Lord, we must find them religiously well-read or instructed. "Attend unto reading; in doing this thou shalt save thyself and them that hear thee," says St. Paul.

But whilst books abound which are admirably adapted to lead us to stamp out sensuality and put on the spirit of Our Lord, the country is flooded, and to their detriment do some know it, with books but too well primed for the destruction of religion and morality in the soul, and for educating their readers in every phase of the most flagrant sensuality. Oh, dear people, what ruinous companions such books are for Christians! The Christian's life-long duty, if he would in more than the name be a follower of Our Lord, is to keep down, to hold within the bounds of right reason, the animal of his nature, and to promote as fully as possible the interests of his soul. Is the person likely to fulfil this all-important duty who fills his mind with the food of sensuality so attractively served up in the soul-dooming volumes that curse society with their presence? Ah, how many there are who have been made utter blanks in practical soul-saving religion! how many are spinning out their life-thread in a demented state as inmates of the asylums of the country! how many are groaning in the eternal regions of reprobation because of the irreligious and immoral poison which they imbibed from wicked books! We sensibly refuse to use food that we have good reason to know will injure the health of our bodies, and why should we not manifest as much good sense in regard to the food of our minds? Time will not permit us to dwell as long and speak as fully on this subject as its great importance demands, but it is safe to say that irreligious and immoral reading is fast sapping religion and morality throughout the country. Catholics should take the alarm and guard their houses against all questionable books and papers, which otherwise will to their grief prove the silent, but sure corruptors of their children. Nor should they neglect, as far as their circumstances will permit, to provide their homes with good, attractive books, and to have as regular visitors one or more of the best Catholic papers. To the shame of some be it said,—and why it is not easy to divine,—they are very reluctant to expend one dollar for a book or a Catholic paper that might be the occasion of rich returns to their children. They spend money freely for things of vastly less importance, whilst aught paid for the home instruction of their families seems to be against their grain. Perhaps if some parents were more generous in providing their homes with good reading material, they would have fewer occasions to deplore the late hours of their sons and daughters. More prudence in making homes attractive would, it is reasonable to suppose, obviate many difficulties which will have, if allowed to continue, no good results on the future lives of some young people. One of the most salutary means to effect this is for parents to aim at cultivating in their children an early taste for good reading, and to instil into them in their tender years a horror for pernicious books and papers, and for the company even of persons who read them. Parents should therefore see to it that their homes are provided with good, wholesome reading matter for their families. In selecting this matter they should have respect to the ages and dispositions of their children. Oh, how many admirable books there are which never fail to entertain children, whilst they impart to them the most wholesome instruction! A nice library of such books would decidedly be one of the most useful acquisitions of the Christian home.

Only those parents who have had experience in this matter can duly appreciate the propriety and merit of what we advocate. To some who have never given the matter of a home library a single thought, the idea may seem of little importance. Yet the family library has always been an important feature of the well-ordered Catholic home. Nor does it require so much of an outlay to be objected to from a pecuniary view, since a very useful collection of books can be procured for a few dollars. These can be added from time to time, and the expense of doing so will not be felt. In this way, after a few years the home will be provided with one of its most valuable features—a well-stocked family library.

Take a broad view of this important and practical subject, at which it is only possible to hint now. It is one that concerns all, but especially parents. Whatever is done in the matter of forming a home library will no doubt be attended with good results. Let all nourish a warm appreciation for good reading, and an absolute horror for such as would lead to evil. Let all hail good books as the best companions, and fly from bad ones as letters from the enemies of religion and morality.

XL.

FIFTEENTH SUNDAY AFTER PENTECOST.

"And in doing so, let us not fail, for in due time we shall reap, not failing."—Gal. vi. 9.

One of the great reasons why the good results produced by sermons and instructions fall vastly short of what might be expected, is that but too many of every congregation receive what is said as a mere matter of theory, without once entertaining a thought that the duty devolves upon them to put it in practice. Sunday after Sunday persons hear their faults pointed out, and are reminded of the virtues which they need, but they go their way, as if what was said did not in the least concern them. It is needless to say that such people are not of the class of the congregation that obey the Apostle's words in our text. They are not of the class that allow the sermons and instructions of the priest to aid them in doing good; they receive not into their hearts the seed of God's word which would fructify unto good; their sinful ways remain unmended, and notwithstanding the good counsel so often imparted to them, they continue to sow so as to reap in eternal woe. It is said indeed that this is the precise case of so many of every congregation. Have we not to deplore this as the practice of too many of this parish? Let us not deceive ourselves; the express object of the sacred writers was to furnish us with the most salutary truths and counsels for our guidance and instruction, and the sermons and explanation on Sundays are intended to bring the hallowed truths home to us so that in our daily lives we may reduce them to practice. Those, and alas! they are many, who fall short of thus utilizing them, invariably fail in well doing, and unfortunately for themselves sow what they will sorely regret to reap. This indifference in respect to what the word of God teaches is an evident sign that those who are afflicted with it are very far from having at heart the end of all religion,—the escaping of eternal misery and the attaining of eternal happiness. When the end is not cherished, the means to this end will not fare better. Those then, who faithfully correspond with the Apostolic mandate not to fail in doing good, so as to sow that they may reap in gladness, are they, as their lives bespeak, who appreciate the vast importance of the end of religion; are they who fully realize that in this world they are between the two extremes, heaven and hell; are they, in fine, who know and feel that in one of these they must spend eternity; and it rests with themselves to decide which. How will they appreciate the value of the word of God, as preached on Sunday, is evinced in their every-day life, which shows forth in practice the good counsel they heard from the lips of the priest? The salutary lessons of the Gospels and Epistles, as they hear them explained, do not pass with them as sterile theory. Like the solicitous bee that flies from flower to flower, extracting from each new substance for its store, they meditate maturely on point after point, and draw therefrom new resources for their promotion in virtue. The matter, not the manner of execution is that which attracts them; they are delighted with the substance, whilst others have no relish save for the shadow. What contributes to the great end, which is wisely the concern of their lives, they most heartily esteem, and since the word of God in sermons and instructions is found by them to be replete with good results, they are always glad to avail themselves of it. Whilst the equals in cleverness of their religiously indifferent neighbors in their respective callings, which they value as the little things of this life, they are as superior to them in what should be the all-absorbing concern of every sensible human being, as good Catholics are to indifferent ones. They are honest in all their dealings, all of which they insist on having in strict harmony with the dictates of their religion; they are truthful, for that religion which they rely on to conduct them to the object of the great concern of their lives, teaches them to spurn all deception. In a word, they are justly regarded in the community in which they live as people in whom confidence can be placed in matters even of the greatest moment, without danger of betrayal. What a blessing to society it would be were the harvest, yielding such people to communities, more generous! Then, indeed, we could disabuse ourselves of untold anxieties in our communications with our fellow-beings.

Let me now ask those that act the indifferent part, who is the more wise,—they who thus have credit before God and man because of the propriety of their lives, besides the continual feast of a good conscience, or they who are deceitful with God and man, and have within the hell of a remorseful, upbraiding conscience? To which of these classes, it is needless to ask, would any sensible man deem it the more honorable before God and man to belong,—to the class made up of those who are Catholics in the discharge of the duties of their state in life, as well as in the discharge of their duties as members of the Church; who are Catholics on week days as well as on Sundays, or to the class composed of those who pose as Catholics at church on Sunday, and on week days are adepts in tricks and disreputable manipulations in their dealings with their fellow-man, and spend their days as little imbued with the spirit of religion as men of no religious pretensions whatever? It is not difficult to divine the answer of every right-minded person in the congregation. Where then is the advantage which those claim who say that their religion should in no way interfere with their business, that it is indeed impossible to be clever and successful in business, and at the same time be a strict Catholic? It should seem that the advantage is on the other side. The man who is truly esteemed for his consistency, honesty, and veracity, surely stands better with the public than one who is, to say the least, suspected of defection in this virtues. If every detail of our dealings with others should be in harmony with the voice of a healthy conscience, then religion must stand by to see it rightly adjusted; if straight business, not dishonest manipulations, is meant, then no reason whatever can be advanced to show that a man's fidelity to the practice of his religion makes him less clever than his indifferent neighbor. All this vaunting that in order to advance himself in the world a man must not allow himself to be embarrassed by religious scruples, is but a cheat and a lie. If a man intends to keep within the bounds of strict honesty, his religion will be no impediment whatever to his advancement; on the contrary his reputation for honesty in his dealings will, I need not say, serve largely to to his advantage. Only those who seek to advance their interests by dishonest and disreputable means, find religion inconvenient, and to such it really is quite inconvenient. We have considered sufficient to lead us to the conviction that the truths imparted and explained on Sundays should be practically utilized in our daily lives, according to the occasion. We have but glanced at the reasoning of those who receive the good counsel given every Sunday, as mere matter of form, and in the glance have seen that they are people who are sowing what one who desires to make himself safe in eternity should hate above all things to reap. A glance, too, we had at the daily life of the man who is always a Catholic, and I challenge anyone to say that his life of all lives is not the one worth living. It has even its reward here, and it will have a never ending one hereafter. Then to obey the advice of the Apostle, it must seem clear that the Sunday explanation of God's word must be treasured up for our good guidance, so that we may not fail in doing good, but may sow in our daily lives what we will be glad to reap when the time for gathering in the harvest will have come.

XLI.

SIXTEENTH SUNDAY AFTER PENTECOST.

" Now to Him who is able to do all things more abundantly than we desire or understand, according to the power that worketh in us: to Him be glory in the Church, and in Christ Jesus, unto all generations, world without end. Amen."—Eph. iii. 21.

These blessed sentiments were zealously penned by St. Paul during his incarceration in a Roman prison. From the devoted and happy feeling evidenced in this text, we should understand that the sufferings and deprivations from which nature of itself would quickly shrink can be undergone and even appreciated by those who faithfully co-operate with the Spirit of God in the cause of good for themselves and others. But too often people who have yet to experience the real consolation of fidelity in God's service, view a life of virtue as full of unbearable circumstances, which render one's life deeply miserable. This is the picture, above all, in which they can find nothing whatever attractive, and the false impression they have of it largely serves to keep them from that line of life demanded of them by the religion which they profess. They allow themselves to be deceived into the impression that in all the scenes which they behold in that picture, they must stand alone and brave, without aid, all the pressures brought upon nature, and therefore swallow large draughts of bitterness without aught of consolation. Though they may not, because of their conceit, express as much, they are not the less of the opinion that those who deny themselves, and comply strictly with the demands of religion, shut out from their lives all enjoyment and sweetness, and commit themselves to unbearable circumstances. Their mistake is in this: they view a life of virtue wholly from a worldly and natural standpoint.

Of their error, St. Paul in our text would disabuse them by his devoted reminder, awaking them to the fact that the mission of every Christian soul is to give glory to God. His happy mood in the midst of his sore trials in the cause of Christ, should serve to show them that He who by His grace enables man to rejoice in being persecuted for His sake, leaves His faithful servant, in the very depths of his soul, a consolation vastly more than earthly. God's true servants have but to dispose themselves in the sorest trials for His action within them, and nature's complaints will be of no avail; they will be experiencing a secret delight, carried forward to do and endure with merit what they would be wholly unequal to, without the power of God. St. Paul's blessed example has been in all ages of the Church imitated by millions, who like him devotedly disposed themselves for the action of God within, and were accordingly carried forward in the cause of Christ far beyond the limits which even the most hopeful could have anticipated. When man thus prepares himself, and continues faithful in his co-operation with God's grace, wonderful, indeed, to those especially who reckon without God, are the works, when the good pleasure of God demands them, which he can carry to a successful issue. He can say with St. Paul: "I can do all things in Him that strengtheneth me."

If, therefore, we would with St. Paul and the millions who have imitated him, give glory to God as children of the Church, we must not listen to the complaints of our corrupt nature, but disabusing ourselves of our sinful self-love, become champions of the cause of God in ourselves and in others, if our position demands it. Thus the designs of God in creating us will be respected. What better is the life of a Christian than that of a pagan if he but follow nature's bent? There are but the two ways open to man: either to devote himself voluntarily to God as all truly Christian people do, or, what too many do to their bitter experience, put himself at the mercy of the whims and bent of his corrupt nature. Quite clear, indeed, is it that there are those who, notwithstanding that Our Lord has pronounced it impossible, pretend to serve the two masters, but all of us know what such a mode of life means—God is not served. So long as we view the lives of true Christians as unattractive and not at all to our taste, it is certain our souls have not yet realized their mission to God, but when we begin by God's grace to conquer the antagonism we find in ourselves, to truly Christian lives, then we commence to glorify God; then we set about to really use as God desires the blessed fruits of Redemption. Ah, how many there are who have not yet really begun! How long will they postpone the glory which they owe to God? how long will they hearken to the whispers of their sinful nature? God grant that they may not delay till it will be too late!

The glory which is unquestionably due to God from all mankind, but especially from the children of the Church, should be tendered to Him, says St. Paul, by all generations. Now, we are of the children of the

Church in this generation, and as such, we should take our part zealously in giving glory to God by lives worthy of our sacred calling as Catholics. This only can we do by a conscientious fidelity to all our Christian duties. In past generations, as well as in this, faithful and unfaithful children have been in the Church. There have been those who, by their co-operation, allowed God's grace to effect in them all which He desired it should, and there have been those who lived as if there being members of the Church implied nothing whatever practical. Could we at this moment interrogate them respecting their circumstances in eternity, who is not prepared to say that their accounts would in truth be vastly different? So, indeed, shall it be when our generation shall have passed away; vastly and consolingly different will be the information which those would be able to give who now allow God's grace to carry them forward in a life of virtue from that which corrupt nature's slaves will have to relate. There are those in this congregation, I am glad to be able to say, who if they continue in their God-blessed fidelity, can be esteemed by their friends on earth after their death as in a position, could they speak, to give the most consoling, the most charming account of their circumstances. There are also those of this parish, and with grief do I say it, who if they continue to obey the promptings of their sinful nature rather than the hallowed teachings of religion, will have a most rueful account. May God grant that they will allow the power of God to work within them before their sentence for the hereafter will be sealed! They have but to will aright and the good God will do the rest. He, in His goodness, created them without their will; He, in His mercy, redeemed them without their will; He, in His love, sanctified them when they were necessitated to have others to vouch for their will; but He, having created them free beings, cannot carry them forward by His grace, save in the co-operation therewith of their wills. Are they not therefore dead to their own best interests, and in fact, ingrates of the very worst type, when they insanely refuse co-operation with God's divine aid? They certainly will not have it in their power to complain that the fault was other than their own, when they discover the result of their ruinous stupidity. Contrary to all that God in His mercy had for them, they continued the willing slaves of their corrupt nature, and for eternity they must rue their evil course.

We perceive the great contrast between those who are nature's slaves and those who have unreservedly given themselves up to God. Let each one here to-day examine himself honestly to see how he stands. If he finds himself really following his own corrupt nature rather than the hallowed teachings of religion, he should quickly make a change, for the longer he remains in his thraldom, the more confirmed it becomes and, by consequence, the more difficult will it be for him to make a change. Let us place no impediment to the grace of God in us, and we will be of the number of this generation who " give glory to God."

XLII.

SEVENTEENTH SUNDAY AFTER PENTECOST.

"One Lord, one faith, one baptism, one God and Father of all, who is above all, and through all, and in us all, who is blessed forever and ever. Amen."—Eph. iv. 6.

How strangely, and not without a sting of reproach, these words of the holy Apostle should sound to those who claim, and they are indeed many, that "it is all the same to which church one belongs, providing, as they put it, he does right." Whose judgment is the man likely to accept who justly values the vast importance of making no mistake in a matter that most gravely bears upon his lot for eternity—St. Paul's, who speaks with the inspiration of God, or the judgment of those who have but little religious sense—a fact which their utterance serves to clearly verify? This question should need no answer. The holy Scriptures are sufficiently clear on the matter, as must appear from our text, and their hallowed teaching, as interpreted by the unerring guide which Christ has given us, has been conscientiously followed by all in every age of Christianity who have really meant to save their souls. Expressions such as that we have adverted to, uttered by people who wish to be esteemed liberal minded, have nothing in them for us, save to convey the impression, not at all ill-founded, that the entertainers of such sentiments are, to say the least, people of very limited religious sense.

What should very much concern us, dear people, is that our lives are, alas! but too often not in keeping with the gift of divine faith. We are as absolutely certain, as that we exist, there is but "one faith," and nothing can possibly be more certain than that as Catholics we profess that faith. Of all this we are as thoroughly satisfied as if, face to face, God had communicated it to us individually; we could never entertain a doubt without contradicting our reason. But the appalling mischief is, that notwithstanding this God-like certainty, not a few of our Catholic people live as if they had no faith. Their faith in theory may be quite all that it should be, yet their daily lives would convey the impression that even this is defective. Granting, however, that their theoretical faith is sound, unless it be reduced to practice it will not serve the purpose of their individual benefit.

Christ Our Lord conferred the divine gift of faith on man for the eternal benefit of all as the children of one family, that individually being responsible for their own salvation, they might, each for himself, reduce it to practice. Each one of us must eventually give an account of the fruit of this divine talent. The end of our faith is that we apply the blessed fruits of redemption to our souls by the practical utilization of the means necessary for salvation which it points out to us, and thereby escape eternal misery and procure everlasting happiness. Only they who thus faithfully comply with its holy teaching will gain the eternal benefit of believing. As for those who, to their shame be it said, scarcely exceed the theory of their faith, they, if death shall overtake them in their unhappy plight, can expect even greater misery in eternity than those who will have lived and died without faith. Catholics content with little more than the theory actually abuse the divine gift of faith, whilst the others refuse to receive it; the former act their evil part in the clear light of the gift, the latter in the darkness of being without it. The servant who accepts his master's money in trust, to be used according to the will of the latter, and not only refuses to comply with the agreement but actually wastes it in the promotion of evil, deserves greater punishment than the servant who disobeyed his master by refusing to accept the money. From this we can, to an extent, perceive the awful misery in eternity which Catholics, who abuse the gift of faith by leading bad lives, can expect. There is in the sacred Scriptures a very striking instance of what shall befall them; I refer to the slothful, unfaithful servant who had not utilized, as his master desired, the talent given him, and "he was bound and cast into exterior darkness." Our blessed Lord intended the parable referred to to illustrate the end of those who will have abused His gifts, and especially the light of divine faith. We should take warning in time, for we know not how soon we may be called upon to render an account of the use we have made of the light of faith which as Catholics we possess.

A protective society which has for its end the guardianship and promotion of the temporal interests of its members, so long as it in no way retards their spiritual interests, is viewed by everyone as a temporal blessing. Now the Church of Jesus Christ is the world-wide divine protective society, which most carefully sees to the spiritual interests of all its members, guards them with a mother's care against every injury, and advances them with a divine skill to the very highest state of perfection. All of us are without the shadow of doubt that our spiritual interests could not possibly have a better nor safer guardian than the one true Church of Jesus Christ; and all of us are absolutely certain that if we but conform to her rules as faithful children, these dearest interests of ours will be safe in life and death. There is not one here, no matter how indifferent his past life may have been, but is thoroughly convinced of this. The indifferent Catholic is quite well aware that the Church is in no way responsible for his ill-becoming life, but that all must be charged to the fact that he has not been a true and faithful member of the Church. How are the indifferent members of reputable societies, which have in view the protection of the material interests of their members, treated? Are their names not stricken from the roll of membership? are they not denied of all the benefits accruing only to those in good standing? You who have been, unfortunately for yourselves, indifferent members of the Church, must see from this very imperfect comparison how stupidly you have neglected your spiritual interests and exposed them to utter and irreparable ruin in eternity. You should shudder at the thought of the danger to which you have exposed yourselves. You must see that unless you are living, faithful members of the Church, the mere name of being of her fold will not save your best interests.

Scarcely necessary, indeed, should it be to refresh our memories with what is demanded of us,— to be true and faithful members of the Church. There is no Catholic but should know that, besides being a member of the body of the Church, he should also be united to her soul. And all should know what this means. What Catholic does not know that the Holy Ghost is the soul of the Church? and what Catholic does not know that to have the Holy Ghost abide in his soul he must be free from mortal sin? These are truths which all of us have been taught from the time that we became capable of receiving instruction. Who will claim that it is not in his power to keep in union with the soul of the Church because of the weakness of his nature and the many incentives to vice with which he is beset? This is the false reasoning of those who love danger and have not yet begun to experience the power of divine grace, which comes from the Sacraments. Without the graces which come from the Sacraments every Catholic knows that it is impossible to keep in union with the soul of the Church, but that with these graces all impossibility vanishes. God is infinitely stonger than our enemies, and when we have His divine grace we have His power with us, and can therefore defy our enemies. No one here, I trust, needs to be informed how easy it is for him to acquire these graces so necessary for his spiritual warfare, by having frequent recourse to the Sacraments of Penance and the Eucharist.

Hence we see, dear people, that the liberal views of some only serve to show that they have little or no religious sense. Nothing can be more certain than that there is but one faith, and that we belong to that faith. The mischief that we have to deplore is that our lives are not, at least always, as consistent as they should be with our belief. We can indeed be of that one faith in theory without being so in practice, which will prove equivalent to having no faith, with this awful difference that we will be accounted the greater criminals before God. With God's grace all without exception can be true and faithful members of the Church, for with St. Paul they will be able to do all which the Church demands of them, " with the grace of Him that strengtheneth them."

XLIII.

EIGHTEENTH SUNDAY AFTER PENTECOST.

"I give thanks to my God always for you, for the grace of God that is given you in Christ Jesus."—I. Cor. i. 1.

A most edifying lesson is taught by the Apostle in the words of our text. For all who will duly bring this teaching home to themselves, the good of their neighbors will be an occasion of their thanks to God. To rejoice at the good of others, whether in body or in soul, and to thank God because He has thus in them given expression of His goodness, is the part of a truly Christian spirit. Thanks to the kind mercy of God, whose divine grace has not failed to people the earth in every age of His Church with millions truly disinterested and Christian, who like the Apostle have made their neighbors good, the occasion of their heartfelt thanks. But, oh! how sad to think of it—the millions that act a contrary part!

Envy, thou bane of human happiness, how large is thy empire! Not the professedly evil alone dost thou hold within thy sway, nor dost thou stop at the followers of false teachers, who, if they could, would destroy every vestige of the tabernacles of God, to erect in their stead those of deluded men, but thou dost even count as your own no small number of these whose Christian profession and duties should shut you from their souls. Ah, it is too true that Catholics there are who allow envy at their neighbor's good to banish peace from their souls. Those there are who cannot brook the contrast between their neighbor's good, the happy consequence of his well-doing, and the evil results of their own ill-conduct. They repine, they are uneasy, not unfortunately for themselves, that good cannot be counted to *their* credit, but because it should be the possession of their neighbor. Had he, like themselves, the grim consequences of ill-doing and neglect of Christian duty to stare him, then indeed no uneasiness should be felt. They grudge their neighbor the merit of his well-doing, whilst they are too fond of gratifying their sinful passions and too slothful to merit for themselves. How vastly better for them it would be should they rather upbraid themselves for their own evil than repine at their neighbor's good, and learn from his example to have good take the place of evil, as the happy result of their fidelity to duty! Are we to number some of those among the envious who, though they have not been wanting in honest and earnest effort, have fallen short of the good results which crowned like efforts on the part of their neighbor? Or are others to be thus numbered whose returns have not been quite so generous as those which serve as occasions of their envy? To them I would say what Our Lord said to those in the Gospel: "Is it not lawful for Me to do what I will? Is thy eye evil because I am good?"

One cannot well fail to see that the lesson taught by the Apostle in the words of our text, was suggested by his perfect love of God and man. Nor can it be difficult to see that envy is directly opposed to this twofold love. When man truly loves God, whatever contributes to His glory, will, far from being an occasion of displeasure, be a reason for his greatest satisfaction. God's gifts, His favors to man, are so many expressions of His goodness and bounty, and therefore they should be eminently calculated to call forth from every Christian a return of gratitude. Is it not meet, then, that the hearts of all true lovers of God should rejoice with St. Paul, and thank Him for drawing the recipients of His gifts more closely to Himself, and exciting within them a disposition of gratitude? How can any true lover of God repine for His being glorified in the person of others? The man in whose heart the love of God is not, would, if he could, stay the bountiful hand of God in respect to his neighbor, and in his churlish selfishness would have all for himself. Not so the man who truly loves God, for whether in himself or in his neighbor the gifts of divine bounty are displayed, he rejoices and thanks the Giver. He is prompted to this, both by his love for God and his love for his neighbor. His heart-felt wish, the offspring of his love in God and for God, of his neighbor, is that every blessing may descend upon him and every prosperity pleasing to God may attend his efforts. Is this not what St. Paul teaches in another place, when he says: " Rejoice with them that rejoice, and mourn with those who mourn" ? What pretensions, therefore, can the man have to the love of his neighbor, who is pained at his good and his prosperity, but enjoys a palpable satisfaction at his misery and his disappointment? Ah, how much there is of this unchristian feeling in the world! And yet all—all, be their color or nation what it may, have the same original parents, have been created to aspire to the same eternal home, and were redeemed by the same most precious blood. Whilst every good can be expected of those who show, with the Apostle, that they truly love God and their fellow-man by thanking the divine Giver for His gifts to the latter, nought but bald wickedness can be expected from the envious. Great God, how numerous is the vile offspring of this withering vice!

Was it not this accursed vice that first introduced murder into the world, by urging one brother to slay another? Has it not always been its history to set brother against brother, friend against friend, and neighbor against neighbor? What but envy set the Pharisees against our blessed Lord, so that nothing short of His life-blood could satisfy their hatred? His own blessed will it was to die for man, and this should have been fulfilled in any case; but they, little knowing the divine will, thirsted for His blood because their envy could not brook the good He did. Where is the man envious of his fellow-man, without hatred and a woful fund of malice, ready to exert itself on every opportunity? Listen to the rash judgers, to the wicked construers of his every word and action; follow the slanderer, the malicious whisperers, and the low, barefaced maligners, and you will have some idea of the extremes to which envy hastens its slave against his neighbor. He hates his fellow-man, and he would fain have all others despise and rise up against him, though his only fault is that he has a good which his envious neighbor has not. It would seem that more than any other vice, envy renders a man fiendlike, by divesting him of every humane feeling towards the one against whom the malice of his vice is directed. Nothing short of his ruin can give him satisfaction. It should be unnecessary to say the unfortunate one, thus devoured with the vice of envy, if he die unhealed of the vice will be eternally excluded from heaven, where only universal love can prevail. Even in this life is the envious man not unfrequently made, by a just judgment of God, drink to its very dregs the bitter cup which he would gladly fill for others.

See then, dear people, how much it becomes us to imitate the blessed example of St. Paul by giving God thanks for the good we perceive in others. By thus conducting ourselves, we make use of the very best safeguard against all manner of envy. This, like many other spiritual defects, is a very subtle vice, and the best way to be certain that it does not lurk in our hearts is to be constant in the practise of the opposite virtue. St. Paul first labored to produce the good in his neighbor, for which he afterwards gave God thanks. We should do likewise, and there is no one, if he tries, but can effect some good in others, for which in sweet charity, which excludes all envy, he can say, "thanks be to the ever good God, who has seen fit to make me the instrument of good to my fellow-man."

XLIV.
NINETEENTH SUNDAY AFTER PENTECOST.

" Wherefore, putting away lying, speak ye the truth every man with his neighbor, for we are members one of another."—Ephes. iv. 25.

One of the most common ways of offending God, of disregarding the rights of others, and of disrespecting one's self is to lack veracity in word or action. " God is truth," and all offences therefore against truth are directly contrary to His good pleasure, and pleasing, of course, to His enemy, the devil, who is the father of lies. It is clear then, that let the end in view be what it may, if only by an untruth it can be attained, to all who have the good pleasure of God at heart, and every Christian should have, it must ever remain unaccomplished. The tender conscience will ever shrink from the merest touch of injured veracity, which of its very nature displeases God, whilst it pleases Satan. Were Christians, were even all practical Catholics possessed of this rich, but too rare blessing, a tender conscience on the matter of veracity, what displeasure the God of truth would be saved, and what a source of real pleasure it would be to have social or business relations with them! As it is, one is constrained to be constantly on his guard so as not to accept as the whole truth in the matter much that he sees and hears, for even those who pass as good and virtuous, very often are wanting in delicacy of conscience on the matter of veracity. It is strange but nevertheless true, that Christians should make so light of a matter which they should know is from its very nature evil, and therefore offensive to God and injurious to their souls. The Catholic with true delicacy of conscience will never lend his tongue to the evil of uttering a deliberate lie, nor will he knowingly be the agent of actions calculated to deceive in aught his fellow-man. His heart, consecrated as every heart should be to the love of his God; his unfeigned Christian regard for his neighbor, which is a necessary outgrowth of his love for God, and his truly Christian self-respect, will ever make him detest the least shadow of untruth.

The reason why so many Catholics, from the youngest even to the oldest, are so wanting in delicacy of conscience on the matter of untruthfulness, is that they seldom or never stop to think of the evil of lying. They falsely think that it is not great harm to tell this little lie, or that slight untruth, and thus the habit grows on them, till at length they hesitate not to lie in matters of importance. To disabuse themselves of the common error of making light of even the least untruth, they should turn from the misleading example of men, and inform themselves of what God's word has to say on the matter. They will not fail to find that without any exception whatever, all lies are condemned and forbidden, and that therefore the slightest untruth is an offence to God, an injustice to their neighbor, and the occasion of disrespect to themselves. Did St. Paul not condemn, in the words of our text, all lying without respect to degrees of malice, and for the reason that every lie of its very nature is evil? His words are very clear: " Wherefore, putting away lying, speak ye the truth every one with his neighbor." Again, we have God's word in another place, forbidding us to be the agents of any manner of untruth: "Be not willing to make any manner of lie." But the sacred Scriptures do not stop at the mere condemnation and forbiddance of all manner of lies; on the contrary, they declare lies even infamous, and pronounce it the strict duty of all to hate them who pretend to truly love God. "A lie is a foul blot in a man.—The just shall hate a lying word." Mark well that no exception is made in these texts of those trifling lies of which even reputed good Catholics are not unfrequently guilty, but like the worst, are condemned and forbidden. God's word is even still more pronounced against lying when it classes, in these words, liars in the category with the worst sinners: "But the fearful, and the unbelieving, and the abominable, and murderers, and the immoral, and idolaters, and *all* liars, they shall have their portion in the lake burning with fire and brimstone, which is the second death."

You see in this sentence *all* liars are passed upon, but it may seem strange to those who constantly make light of certain lies, which they have ever deemed of no great harm, that their case should be so formidable. The matter needs but little explanation. The custom of telling small lies is hateful to God, and provokes Him to hold back from the soul the special graces which otherwise He would have bestowed upon her, and which she may need to keep from mortal sin. Besides, the person whose love for God is so weak and defective as not to prevent him from offending God by *light* lies, is not likely to have sufficient love for Him to abstain from *grievous* ones, should the occasion of being guilty of them present itself. It is the well-known experience of sinners that habits of vice have begun by the commission of small faults, but ended in extremes. From this we can easily conceive the mistaken, the unchristian reasoning of those who think it is no great harm to tell a little lie, when if they were truly religious people, no motive whatever could induce them to deviate from truth. No matter how exalted the end, if only by the telling of a little lie it can be attained, the forfeit is too great for the conscience of the truly good Christian. The evil done to God by the least untruth is too great for the reparation which even the greatest good thus effected could make. As well as being evil of itself, a lie, like other sins, has its degree of malice, and this varies according to the gravity of the matter. If it be directed against a virtue necessary for salvation, or should it have for its aim serious injury to a neighbor, then it would be a grave sin. Also, it should not be forgotten, that though a lie be not directed against any necessary virtue, and though it be in no way caculated to inflict direct injury on others, yet should it be to them the occasion of serious scandal, this of itself would be sufficient to make the one who tells it guilty of mortal sin; or where scandal need not be feared, the case would be the same should the teller of a venial lie call upon God by an oath to witness his untruth.

From these few hints, dear people, it must seem clear to any one present that his duty to his God, his neighbor, and himself, combine to teach him to be truthful in all his words and actions. He should perceive the very great danger untruthfulness foreshadows, even though it be confined for the time to what he may be pleased to call small matters. We have seen that from small beginnings habitual vice takes its rise, and that the habit of lying confines itself, not to small matters, but as the occasion presents itself, hurries its victim into the shadows of deadly guilt. We have also adverted to the awful portion which God's word avers is in store for all those who commit themselves to the vice of lying. Should it not then appear to us very proper to examine our daily lives to see wherein we may be at fault, and manfully set about a conscientious reformation? Means are not wanting to us. The first, it would seem, we should resolve upon constantly using, is to ever bear in mind the injury we do to God, our neighbor, and ourselves, by every untruth; the second, the good that accrues to us from always telling the truth; and the third is to pray to God for strength ever to hate a lie, remembering that "the mouth that lieth killeth the soul."

XLV.

TWENTIETH SUNDAY AFTER PENTECOST.

"And be not drunk with wine, wherein is luxury, but be ye filled with the Holy Spirit."—Eph. v. 18.

Besides its sad effect in common with other grievous sins, which is the destruction of the life of grace in the soul, drunkenness extinguishes for the time the light of reason, and makes a rational being a mere fossil. It leaves its victim graceless and irrational, a state certainly most deplorable for a human being, even for a short time. He who with God's grace in his soul was almost the rival of the angels, cannot in drunkenness be considered a rival of the lowest species of the brute creation. The latter has its instinct, its normal guide, but no guide whatever has the man who is really drunk; like an insane person, his brain is on fire and all his worst passions come to the surface. The meanest passions of his nature supersede grace, reason, and all his good qualities, and carry the man not unfrequently to the irretrievable extremes—death and hell. Who could expect of him, whilst in that sad plight of self-inflicted insanity, anything worthy of a man, and much less of a Christian man? For the gross gratification of a beastly appetite, the man, the Christian, who wilfully drinks unto drunkenness, forfeits all the most noble prerogatives of a man and a Christian, and sinks himself into a state most reversive of the designs of

God in creating him. Oh! what a misery; what a burning shame for men, aye, Christian, Catholic men, that this self-sought degradation is so common among them! that position, education, and even the hallowed teachings of religion are so often set at nought for the gratification of this vile and worse than beastly passion for intoxicating drink! Search the regions of God's justice in eternity; canvass the various grades of society throughout the world, and then ask yourself whether drunkenness is not to be numbered, in our day at least, as one of the most terrible and effectual instruments which the powers of darkness use to frightful advantage to keep souls out of heaven, and spread misery and ruin upon the face of the earth, or in other words, to bring temporal and eternal ruin to men! Once this wretched passion for intoxicating drink gets control of a man, he no longer reasons with the wisdom of a man; he is swayed by his appetite, which bids a ready defiance to all reasoning. " Wine is a luxurious thing, and drunkenness riotous; whosoever is delighted therewith shall not be wise." (Prov. xx. 1). Ah, how many can rue that day in which they first experienced delight in the vile cup, which was for them the beginning of the dread disease which eventually sapped all the manliness and Christianity in them, and reduced them to their present degraded and unhappy condition, that of besotted animals! " Wo to you that rise up early in the morning to follow drunkenness, and to drink till the evening to be inflamed with wine." (Isa. v. 11). It should be remembered that the woes of the sacred Scriptures are uttered against those who drink large quantities without becoming drunk, and they are legion, as well as against those who grossly succumb to drunkenness.

"Wo to you that are mighty to drink wine, and are stout men at drunkenness." (Isa. v. 22). Though not utterly drunk, they live befogged and influenced by liquor, so that for the most part it is the latter, not the man, that gives origin to much that they do and say. It is quite unnecessary to remark that it is anything but agreeable to transact business with men who are, from the effects of liquor, befogged and in an abnormal state. Who that has had experience of an instance, will not solemnly protest against a repetition, not so much indeed, though sufficient, for the immediate disagreeableness, as for the well-known lack of consistency and principle which but too often are the concomitants of such a state! The most awful evil, because irremediable, however, of all the misery which habitual excess in drinking brings upon its unfortunate victim, is his eternal exclusion from the kingdom of heaven. Nothing can be more clearly expressed than this is in the sacred Scriptures. It is too bad that the voice of the Scriptures, though so full of awful meaning against the vice of drunkenness, is so often neglected for arguments which ought to have far less weight, at least with Christians, by those who would correct their neighbor, and that it is so little heeded by those who should reform. What should have more weight with Christians who are unfortunately addicted to this vice, than God's word telling them that by it they destroy the life of grace in their souls, they rob themselves of every healthy sentiment of religion, they act the desperate part of tempters of the almighty God, and finally insanely exclude themselves from eternal happiness, and plunge themselves into everlasting misery? Oh! that men, who have for the sake of the gross gratification which the betraying cup has afforded them, been flinging from them all that is most dear to them in time and eternity, would bring home to themselves and allow to sink deep into their hearts these sentiments of the Scriptures: " Be not deceived; neither fornicators, nor idolaters, nor adulterers, nor drunkards, shall possess the kingdom of heaven." (I. Cor. vi. 9). Behold, O unfortunate Christian, who besots yourself by excess in drinking, God's unerring word classes you with idolaters, and intoxicating drink is the god of your idolatry! Before Heaven you stand in the debasing category of the gross idolater; in time and in eternity, if you continue the slave of drink, you will be his companion in misery. The words of men you may indeed explain away; God's words must abide, for "heaven and earth shall pass away, but His word shall not pass away;" of this, the preface to the foregoing text reminds you in these words, "be not deceived," as much as to say: what I have to announce is the whole truth, and nothing but God's truth. This is the truth, O Christian, addicted to excess in drinking, which classes you for time and eternity, unless you mend your ways, with idolaters! Is the animal pleasure which drink affords you, worth the tremendous sacrifice? What a sacrifice for a Christian to sink into an animal life, which must, as sure as the great God exists, end in hell! You may have pretensions to religion, but the truth is, so long as you are given to excess in drinking, the animal prevails over the spirit, and the sad consequence is an animal, not a religious life, is what you lead, all your best pretensions to a religious life to the contrary notwithstanding. The heart of man must sacrifice to God, and not to His creatures; till this is effected, a man's religion is but merest deception. The heart of the man who has the accursed habit of drinking to excess is given to intoxicating liquor rather than to God, and no matter how manifest or pronounced his religious pretensions, his life is without merit. Hear God's word, and be not contented with mine as a conclusive argument. "Now the works of the flesh are manifest, which are fornication, uncleanness, drunkenness, revellings, and such like, of which I foretell you, as I have foretold you, that they who do these things shall not obtain the kingdom of heaven." (Gal. v. 19). Could words be clearer than these? Are they not a direct proof of my claim that so long as a man is given to excess in drinking he is on no higher grade than that of an animal life, be his pretensions to religion which they may? Ah, how often this animal life and no merit are concealed by a religious exterior! Guard, O men! against the habit of this degrading vice, for when once contracted it is most difficult to correct. For you who must confess the habit you unfortunately have, mark well what I say: there is but one true and lasting remedy, and that is God's divine grace. A thousand times more weight with me would it be to know that a man addicted to drinking to excess had really resolved to give his heart to God in the earnest practice of his religious duties, and had followed that resolution up by frequent receptions of the Sacraments, and a *settled daily devotion*, than to hear of his making any number of pledge promises, so very often idle, at temperance meetings. The grand secret of the vast good done by the saintly Father Matthew was not in his eloquence, was not in his arguments, was not even in the pledge he gave, but verily was in this: he led the people whom he pledged to give their hearts to God in the practice of their religious duties. Till the affections of the heart are transferred from the creature to God, and God's grace is sought and co-operated with, a man may seem to reform, but there can be no true, radical reformation.

XLVI.

TWENTY-FIRST SUNDAY AFTER PENTECOST.

"And take unto you the helmet of salvation, and the sword of the Spirit (which is the word of God).—Eph. vi. 17.

Like the Israelites in the desert are we in this world; they were on their way to the land of promise, so are we; they were sustained by miraculous food from heaven, so are we; and their courage failed them not so long as they maintained the hope of reaching the object of their pursuit; neither will ours fail us whilst we keep our hope alive. We are journeying to eternity, and if true to the end for which God started us on the way, we must have our aspirations centred on the promised kingdom, and our Moses must be Jesus. The stronger our hope, the truer we are to our divine Leader; and the greater the esteem we entertain for the object of our journey, and the more thoroughly we relish the sustenance from heaven, the more acceptable to God will be our hope. Only when they forgot the object for which they journeyed, and thereby allowed their hope to cool, did the Israelites surrender to the tempter, and basely sigh for the flesh-pots of Egypt. This, too, alas! is the great reason of the vast sway which the powers of darkness have but too generally among Christians. They, unfortunately, live in sad forgetfulness of that kingdom, the like of which, says St. Paul: "Neither eye hath seen, ear heard, nor heart of man conceived," and therefore their hope becomes cool, or perhaps quite dead. Hence the enemy finds no great difficulty in inducing them to barter it for the trifles and vicious objects which he delusively holds out to them. Knowing this, the Apostle admonishes us " to take unto us the helmet of salvation," which is no other than our Christian hope. The absolute necessity of this part of our Christian armor is abundantly apparent from what we have considered, and the striking significance of the figurative name by which the Apostle has designated it. Our heads and our hearts must be protected against the attacks of our enemies; the helmet of hope must serve the purpose for the former, and the word of God for the latter. This sword of the word Our Lord teaches us how to use.

One of the most remarkable expressions of Our Lord's infinite zeal to instruct us in everything pertaining to our salvation, is His most astonishing condescension in allowing Himself to be tempted by the devil. "Jesus was led by the Spirit into the desert, to be tempted by the devil," (Matt. iv. 1). Even if we had not this text to show us that it was Our Lord's blessed will to be tempted, we should know that the devil, a mere creature, had no power to tempt Him, only in so far as He was pleased for our expressed instruction to grant it to him. What a source of instruction the nature of the temptations and the manner in which Our Lord met them must be to all who seriously give their minds to the study of them! Not until He was hungry, after His fast of forty days and as many nights, did He permit the devil to begin his series of temptations, thereby for our great instruction affording him all the advantage possible. Though not so in Our Lord, in whom there could be no concupiscence, that was about the stage in which our inferior nature would incline to desperation, and be most susceptible to attacks from the enemy; therefore He selected it. The devil knew of the long fast of Our Lord, and he also knew of His hunger, hence he assailed Our Lord by tempting Him not to bide His time till He should procure food in the ordinary way, but to make use of His almighty power to procure bread to satisfy His hunger. Our Lord met his temptation by telling him: "It is written. Not in bread alone doth a man live, but in every word that proceedeth from the mouth of God." (Matt. iv. 4). Bread but ministers to the life of the body, man's inferior part, whilst God's word sustains the life of the soul, the superior part of man. But at the suggestion of the devil and contrary to God's written word, to satisfy the body as is done by, alas! only too many who observe not the fast of precept, would be to starve the superior part for the gratification of the inferior. This is to take a narrow view of the abuse. May we not truly say that every one who knowingly fails to obey the voice of the Scriptures, informing him that it is his duty " to mortify by the Spirit the deeds of the flesh," or " to put on the spirit of Our Lord Jesus Christ," which is pre-eminently a spirit of self-denial and mortification, gratify the flesh at the expense of the spirit, and thereby waive the salutary warning of God's word and comply with the seductions of the tempter? This was the deplorable abuse that covered the face of the earth when Our Lord came to walk as the God-man among men. How is it in the age in which we live? Are not the large majority of the inhabitants of the earth composed of those who either publicly or silently disregard the teaching of God's word and live the willing dupes of the tempter? Are they not even wresting the word to their destruction by accepting the tempter's interpretation of it? It was to teach us that even the very word itself will the archenemy pervert to assail us, that Our Lord permitted the devil to tempt Him by the word of God: "If thou be the Son of God, cast thyself down," for it is written: "That He hath given His angels charge over thee, and in their hands shall they bear thee up, lest perhaps thou dash thy foot against a stone." Oh, what havoc of souls has he wrought by this perversion of the sense of God's word! Oh, the millions who have gone into eternity after wasting, nay, cursing their lives, by following his soul-dooming guidance, in his perversion for their ruin of the sense of the sacred Scriptures! the millions that are now following in their footsteps in the same unhappy fashion! They have deplorably failed to learn from the instruction of Our Lord when He taught them to reject the evil one's false interpretation. His answer to the evil one should have taught them that to follow his interpretation was to tempt God: "It is written again: Thou shalt not tempt the Lord thy God." Hence then, to prove a sword against our spiritual enemies, the word of God must be accepted by us in no other sense than that in which He intended it; and to be absolutely certain that thus we have it, we must heed no other interpreter than the divine and infallible one He has given us—His Church. Coming from her infallible lips, it is as God intended, a two-edged sword, whilst from other lips it can for good become the occasion of perversion to many as the conduct of the professors of so-called Christianity but too clearly shows.

That the word of God may serve as a two-edged sword in the warfare against our spiritual enemies, we must hear it and allow its teaching to produce good fruit in our daily lives. This we will not fail to do if we be fully convinced of its vast importance as a means of defence against our common enemies, the devil, the world, and the flesh. The way to arrive at this conviction is to keep constantly in view the great stress which Our Lord, the Apostles, and the Saints, have laid upon our duty to hear and keep the word of God. One of the chief works of Our Lord was to preach, and He sent His ministers to continue that work till the end of time. All the Saints, as their works and lives show, have been unanimous in their estimate of the importance of reading the word of God in good books. Why, I ask, did Our Lord labor so hard in preaching? Why, again, did He leave the preaching of the word of God a most incumbent duty on His ministers? And why, in fine, have the Saints been so unanimous in regard to the importance of religious reading? Should we not see from all this, dear people, the vast importance of hearing, and reading, and keeping, by serious thought, the word of God? There is no temptation that will prevail against us if we, in fidelity to the instruction of Our Lord, but fortify ourselves with God's word. The "helmet of salvation" will be verily what its name bespeaks in our regard, so long as we keep ourselves well armed with the sword of the word of God; and thus armed we will not fail to be if we fulfil our duty as Catholics in hearing, and reading, and keeping God's word. "Blessed are they who hear the word of God and keep it."

XLVII.

TWENTY-SECOND SUNDAY AFTER PENTECOST.

"For God is my witness, how I long after you all in the bowels of Jesus Christ."—Phil. 1. 8.

An admirable lesson is taught in these words of the Apostle, and it is the duty of every good Christian to learn and practice it in respect to his fellow-man. The tender charity which the apostolic utterance denotes for the spiritual well-being of all is, alas! too little known and practised in even the Christian, nay, we must say it, Catholic world. No Christian, whose instruction has been all it should be, doubts his obligation to hold out the hand of charity to his neighbor, be his religion, his color, or his nationality what it may, when he is in temporal want, and it is in his power to come to his assistance. Why then should any Christian doubt his still more serious obligation to tender assistance, when the opportunity affords itself, to his neighbor in spiritual want? How can the conscientious Christian Catholic fail to see that since his neighbor's circumstances in the latter case are by far the more desperate, and forebode the worst possible calamity, his obligation is proportionately the more grave? The three persons of the Most Blessed Trinity, the Queen of heaven and earth, the angels and saints, and even the poor suffering souls in Purgatory, interest themselves in their respective ways in the salvation of man, and shall good

Christians, who live side by side, or in the same community with their indifferent co-religionists, with whom their influence is not a little, waive as no part of their duty to utilize opportunities for their best spiritual interests? To act thus cannot seem right or in keeping with the charity which the Apostle would teach us in to-day's Epistle, in the opinion of anyone who will give the matter serious thought. But whilst an obligation of this nature devolves upon all good Christians, there are those who because of their position, relation, or circumstances with regard to others, have respecting them a special obligation under this head.

Of these, parents and guardians, on account of the vast importance of their duty with regard to children whom Providence commits to them, should by all means head the list. The first duty of parents and guardians is to be God-fearing and law-abiding themselves. If they neglect their duty to God, and observe not His law or that of His Church, their vile example will be, alas! but too well copied by their children. As parents have been the instruments of God in bringing their children into life, on them the responsibility largely devolves to aid in preparing them for that better life in eternity. The child is father to the man, for the bringing up of the child foreshadows the man that religion and society may expect. How vast, therefore, is the importance of religion and society that every home should be presided over by good, conscientious parents! A good way to know the Christian parents who are quite far from being good and conscientious in any parish is to note the vile conduct of their children. Exceptions there indeed are; good parents may sometimes have wayward children, but the rule is, when the conduct of children is bad, all is not right at home. How often we see these words of Scripture verified: "The child that is left to his own will, bringeth his mother to shame"! Had the parents done their duty, in nine cases out of ten those children would be their glory instead of their shame. The children must suffer for the criminal neglect and, in many cases, ill-teaching conduct of their parents, and it is well if their misfortune will end with this life. The human so-called law, which is so often at variance with the divine, and is so often framed without respect for religion, the self, or society, allows the parent who has thus cursed society with not only useless but vile members, to pass with impunity and even as an object of pity. Not so with a just God, who will hold parents to a most strict account for their abuse of His confidence in their neglect of duty in bringing up their children. Their neglect to instruct their children; their neglect to watch over them; their neglect to correct them; their neglect to pray for them, and finally, their neglect to give them good example, will all be met by just punishment. Not only do parents owe this duty of charity, and it may be said of justice, to their children, but for their own and their children's sakes to each other. The mother of the family should do whatever may be in her power, and mothers of merit have no small influence, to have the father's example worthy of the imitation of his children, and the father, the family head, in like manner has the same obligation towards the mother. If the conduct of either be such as is not calculated to edify the children, it will have a very telling effect in counteracting the good teaching of the correct parent. Not only, therefore, are parents constrained by their mutual obligation of charity to contribute to each other's spiritual betterment, but also on account of their duty towards their children. In line with the obligation of parents towards their children is that of Christians in authority in respect to those under them. They should see that Catholics under them practise their religion. Whilst many motives, arising from their own personal interest, could be advanced here as a recompense for their solicitude, their obligation of charity is all that we can afford time to ask them to fully appreciate. The other motives will be touched on at another time. We should know that it is idle to pretend to love God whilst we lack charity, especially the species in question, towards our neighbor. What then will it avail for a person in authority to keep up an exterior devotion, whilst they egregiously neglect to use their influence to have Catholics under them practise their religion? Oh, how many Catholic employers are as indifferent concerning the Catholics under them as if they had no duty to reprimand them for their views and neglect of their religious obligations! There is, sad to say, too much of this real, uncharitable conduct displayed by Catholics for which, before God, they are responsible and will pay the penalty. Oh, the millions that are constantly engaged in ruining souls, by leading them into every phase of vice, and the few, very few, who are willing to offer a single opportune word towards saving even their erring friends! No doubt many who have thoughtlessly enlisted in the ranks of dangerous companions, and but too often found among them their temporal and eternal ruin, might have been saved had their better acquaintances or friends acted the charitable part by putting them on their guard in time. A false delicacy and indifference are the two great impediments which prevent so many Catholics from taking an interest in the reformation of their weaker brethren. On account of these, they forever leave their obligation of charity unfulfilled, and allow to run to their ruin persons whom by timely advice they might indeed have saved. Would they concede that those they so uncharitably neglect would fulfil their duty towards them, had their relative conditions been different? They certainly could not. Why then do they so often deceive themselves and their confessor by not making their uncharitable conduct in this matter a notable part of their confession, when they seek the grace of the Sacraments? Oh, the awful rigor which God will one day exercise towards many for their accursed false delicacy and indifference respecting the discharge of this important duty!

In conclusion then let me say, dear people, whether you be parents, guardians, persons in authority, or otherwise, God holds you bound to show an interest in the spiritual welfare of your neighbor, by doing what charity and prudence may suggest when the occasion presents itself. Thus you will practice that high and to God, very pleasing branch of charity, which the blessed words of St. Paul are calculated to teach.

XLVIII.

TWENTY-THIRD SUNDAY AFTER PENTECOST.

"Be followers of me, brethren, and observe them who walk so as you have our model."—Phil. iii. 17.

In this sentence the Apostle teaches that one of the duties of those who would truly serve God, is to keep constantly in mind a correct model for imitation. He had continually before his mind the divine Model, and feeling confident that as far as man could, he had succeeded in reflecting in his life that sublime exemplar, he called upon those whom he addressed to follow him. Now as the first condition of true discipleship of our blessed Lord is self-denial, to perfection in this St. Paul ardently aspired, and he unquestionably attained all the success possible to man. From this, all his other brilliant virtues followed. If we would obey the exhortation of the Apostle, then we should also aspire to perfection in self-denial, for thus only can we be followers of him as he was of Our Lord.

The end of self-denial is the destruction, as far as possible, of damning self-love, and the building upon its ruins of a saving love of self. The divine example of Our Lord, and the faithful reflection of it in the blessed life of St. Paul, teach saving self-love, whilst all who aspire not to imitate the self-denying life of Our Lord and His Apostle, whatever may be their pretensions, are but slaves, in its varied phases, of damning self-love.

Of them the Apostle speaks in these words: "For many walk, of whom I have told you often (and now tell you, weeping) that they are enemies of the cross of Christ; whose end is destruction: whose God is their belly: and whose glory is their shame: who mind earthly things." (Phil. iii. 18). These words apply to-day as they did in the time of the Apostle, not only to the slaves of passion without, but especially to certain Catholics in every parish. We have them in this community to our grief, and, alas! only too many. To trace their daily lives would be to find them utterly wanting in practical religion, and deplorably filled with the accursed offspring of a rank, damning self-love. In a word, we would find them utter strangers to all, or at least most of their Christian duties, and adepts of vice in its varied degrees of malice. The innate desire for happiness, which has place in them as in every human creature, is not directed to the object to which the self-denying life of Our Lord and His Apostle point, but verily to the gross, degrading swine-husks of passion. They yearn for happiness, but they turn from the living to seek it amongst the dead; they stupidly refuse to use the only means to attain it, and anxiously plunge themselves into vice, which embitters their lives and makes them a burden and a reproach. Impossible is it for man to attain that happiness for which he craves, in this world and the next, save by imitating the best Christian masters who, after our blessed Lord, are St. Paul, his apostolic brethren, and their saintly followers of every age of the Church. The first essential lesson which these great masters teach is self-denial, and the more perfect we become in this, the nearer we approach the desired object. The necessity, then, for human happiness, in time and in eternity, of self-denial is clear; but in what, it may be asked, does it consist?

To answer this question with a view to benefit each one in particular, I will ask each one here to look into his daily life, and remember that what he finds there, which is not in harmony with his duty as a Christian, must be corrected. In this correction self-denial consists. He will doubtless find sins of a positive and of a negative nature; he will find internal or spiritual sins, and those that are external. To correct them is his first step in self-denial. Reading or companionship dangerous to faith and morals; all profane language and want of filial love for parents; breaches of charity against our neighbor; thoughts and desires, words and actions contrary to chastity; dishonesty and false testimony are sins of a positive nature; and every neglect of Christian duty, such as prayer, fast and abstinence, hearing of Mass on Sundays and days of obligation, and the reception of the Sacraments, not only as often as the precept requires, but as frequently as our spiritual need will suggest, is considered negative sinning. At the bottom of this neglect, in most cases, can be found the bane of practical religion, spiritual sloth. All who are guilty of sins in any of these ways are, in proportion to the extent of their positive or negative defects, wanting in Christian-like self-denial, or in other words are the victims of a damning self-love. But we have yet to give thought to even more subtle, and therefore more dangerous work of sinful self-love.

One needs but to give close attention to what passes in his interior to perceive in what a marked degree the animal instincts of his weak nature assert themselves there. It is the work of self-denial to refine, polish, and reform whatever may be in these interior motions which, as he finds them, cannot be reconciled with a love of self that has God for its end. Within, we have in our persons God's divine likeness, hence if we would do God honor in the temple of our souls, we must be careful to eliminate, by self-denial, whatever is not in accordance with His good pleasure. Pride must give place to humility; self-conceit, self-sufficiency, and presumption must be succeeded by a healthy confidence in God. If in the past, as is too often the case, we find that we have been carried hither and thither by the whims of a mercurial curiosity, and judged and weighed matters, not according to the maxims of the Gospel, but after the fashion of the world, self-denial must correct all this by showing forth in our persons, at all times and under all circumstances, a truly Christian spirit. The Gospel of our divine Model should ever be recognized as our true and sure guide under all circumstances. To this standard, if she be truly refined by self-denial, will the Christian soul carry all the cases presented by memory and imagination, and there strip them of all that by which sinful self-love conceals the dangerous effects of which they are capable. But before this happy consequence can be reached, the will, which is the mistress of the other powers of the soul, must be by self-denial conformed to order. If this be neglected we can never hope to succeed in attaining a well ordered interior. I speak of that will power in man of which, from time to time, we hear great boasting. Of itself, it is capable of nothing for salvation, but with the grace of God aiding and accompanying its efforts, it is the motor of all meritorious action. Co-operating with grace, it has in every age of the Church produced the greatest saints, but of itself, and refusing to use this divine gift, it has cursed the earth with every species of wickedness and with men who have been the disgrace of humanity. It is of the human will in this sense that the sacred Scriptues speak when they say: "Go not after thy lusts, but turn away from thy own will; if thou give to thy soul her desires, she will make thee a joy to thy enemies." "The child that is left to his own will bringeth his mother to shame."

We see then, from the consideration of these few points, the vast importance of imitating St. Paul in his interior and exterior self-denial. This twofold self-denial is precisely that which distinguishes the true followers of Our Lord from those who are but Christians in name. Clear, indeed, is this from the words of Christ: "If any man will come after Me, let him deny himself, and take up his cross and follow Me." Hence as St. Paul did, so must we do; he denied himself and carried his cross; so must we. Then we will be followers of him as he was of Christ, and each of us can say with him, "I live now, not I, but Christ liveth in me." (Gal. ii. 20).

XLIX.

TWENTY-FOURTH SUNDAY AFTER PENTECOST.

"Giving thanks to God the Father, who hath made us worthy to be partakers of the lot of the saints in light."—Col. i. 13.

Amongst the many gifts for which Catholics should thank God is especially that of divine faith, without which all His other favors, though indeed deserving of eternal thanks, would not avail them, or rather would contribute to their eternal woe by rising up in judgment against them. It is this divine gift then, which when utilized as God wills, makes all the other precious favors of God, and they are many, fruitful to each individual soul. "Without faith it is impossible to please God," and when man's life fails to afford pleasure to God, it is an utter blank, supernaturally speaking. From this, therefore, we should understand the inestimable value of the gift of divine faith, and by consequence the incumbency of the duty that constantly devolves upon us of tendering God thanks for the blessed boon. At no time do we value so highly the convenience and safety of a sufficiency of good food as when for a time we have suffered its want, or when at least we learn of the pangs endured and the ghastly deaths brought on by the want of it in famine-stricken countries. So, too, would we better realize the infinite goodness of God towards us had we, like so many others, been for a time without faith, or when, by reading and hearing, and seeing, we make ourselves acquainted with the sad lot of those who have no faith, or that of these little less sad who have next to no faith, for "they are cast about by every wind of doctrine," and rely on the opinions of erring men for the so-called faith that is in them. They are, indeed, in a spiritual sense, and therefore the more to be deplored, famine-stricken. Have we some among us who were once spiritually famine-stricken for want of the food of God's truth, but now, thanks to God, enjoy the rich plenty of the household of the faith? They indeed can testify to the great goodness of God towards us who have never been in want, just as he who once suffered great hunger of body knows best how to appreciate the blessing of a sufficiency of food.

It is the every day duty of man, with a grateful heart to tender thanks to God for all His divine gifts, but especially should this duty be conscientiously discharged for the gift of faith, which lends supernatural value, when practically corresponded with to the life of its possessor. There is no salvation without divine faith, for Our Lord has said "He that believeth and is baptized, shall be saved; but he that believeth not, shall be condemned." When, therefore, we give thought to the many who pretend to have no faith, even in the existence of the true God, in Jesus Christ His divine Son, nor in His divine doctrines, and all because of the fault of their ancestors, who through vice lost sight of divine revelation; when we consider the millions who pass as Christians, but for want of Baptism are not the millions who are indeed Christians, contenting themselves with detached fragments of Christianity, on account of the defection of their forefathers, who abandoned the one true Church, we can form some idea of how much it becomes us to be thankful that we are the children of the Catholic Church, which holds the deposit of divine faith. God has done them no injustice; they have been placed at a cruel distance from the truth by consequence of the malicious defections of their forefathers. They must make their way to the truth or be lost, and if the latter, they will be constrained to condemn themselves for all eternity as their own destroyers, for God will afford them ample opportunity to reach the blessed boon of faith. See in all this, dear people, the great reason we indeed have for heartfelt thanks to God, who by special graces, which He was in no way constrained to give, preserved our forefathers from all defection in the true faith of Jesus Christ, as taught by our holy Mother, the Church. Oh, how vastly more favorable our circumstances are to reach heaven, than theirs! How touchingly pitiable is the benighted condition of the poor Jews! how sadly degrading, how wretchedly gloomy that of the poor heathens, and what obstacles so telling on weak human nature are in the way of those who are " cast about by every wind of doctrine," and constantly plied with the most malicious lies, and stultified by every phase of the most blatant bigotry against the one true Church, by designing people whose bad faith is only too often responsible for their hatred of the truth! So far we have been trying to realize the incumbency of our duty to thank God for the gift of faith by comparing our advantages, as children of the Church, with the woful disadvantages of those who are not of the divine fold. We should not forget, however, before we end our thoughts on the subject, to re-

member, as we remarked in the beginning, that all
our other gifts from on high depend on our faith for
their fruitfulness.

No matter how great may be the natural accomplishments and talents of a human being, without faith
it is impossible for him "to please God." The soul
blessed with divine faith, and hope, the younger sister,
when these virtues are religiously alive, also enjoys that
divine virtue from which the two former and all others
draw their life—divine charity. Thus enriched with
these three virtues in the full vigor of their fruitfulness, every good possible to man in his respective circumstances can be expected. For where faith, hope,
and charity are, there too is sanctifying grace; and
where the latter is, there also are the beautiful moral
virtues, like so many delicate flowers, making the garden of the soul pregnant with the fragrance of heaven.
With practical faith as the soil, lively hope as the rich
outgrowth, and ardent charity as the divine dew of
heaven, without which the soil would be utterly barren, the moral virtues never fail to cluster throughout
the spiritual garden, as so many expressions of the
super-excellence of the soil when moistened by the
divine dew of charity. To all this the Holy Ghost in
His infinite bounty adds spiritual gifts, and these gifts
are not without fruits, and to complete the rich
beauty of the spiritual inclosure, He diffuses a light,
the delicate mellowness and resplendency of which are
beyond the power of man to describe. See then, my
dear people, how much we Catholics have to be thankful for in the blessed boon of divine faith. Oh, how
our hearts should glow with the most sincere gratitude
when we think on the absolute necessity of divine

faith to please God and save our souls; when we consider our advantages as compared with the millions without the pale of the Church; and when, in fine, we dwell on the blessed boon of practical faith itself from which, as from its foundation, arises all the supernatural good to be found in man here below! We should never forget that the most acceptable expression of our gratitude to God will be to conform our daily lives to the teaching of our Mother, the Church, for thus only will we be "partakers of the lot of the saints" on earth, and effectually prepare to be partakers of their glory hereafter. The flowers of the garden of the soul must be seen to be duly appreciated, so that attracting, they may impress and edify our less fortunate neighbors, and thereby result in no slight good to them. Oh, what untold good the correct lives of good Catholic men and women are capable of effecting in their non-Catholic brethren, and how well they fulfil their duty of gratitude to God for the sacred gift of faith by honoring the gift in the daily practise of virtue! Believe me, dear people, the ill-becoming lives of some Catholics are responsible in no slight degree for many remaining out of the Church, whilst the edifying lives of correct members of the Church the world over are largely contributing to turn the tide towards the Church, which of late we can contemplate with so much satisfaction. Good lives on our part are by far the best arguments with which to induce our non-Catholic neighbors to seek the "light of the saints," and are eminently the best way to thank God for the gift of faith.

www.ingramcontent.com/pod-product-compliance
Lightning Source LLC
Chambersburg PA
CBHW021352230426
43666CB00006B/503